GIVE *and be Rich*

"This book has changed how I feel about myself and others. I would recommend *Give and Be Rich* to anyone who wants to know how easy it can be to feel like a million bucks without costing anything but kindness."

— **Brian Dreger**

"In this incredible book Give and be Rich Penny's heart wisdom is so much more than words. Within are true gifts for you, that when fully received, will unlock the next level of enlightenment on your journey toward the riches that you've been waiting for. Golden Blessings…"

— **Bob & Betty Ann Golden**, Eagle Distributors, Master Certified Trainers, SendOutCards

GIVE
and be
Rich

TAPPING THE CIRCLE OF ABUNDANCE

PENNY TREMBLAY

NEW YORK

GIVE *and be Rich*
TAPPING THE CIRCLE OF ABUNDANCE

© 2014 PENNY TREMBLAY.

Published in New York, New York, by Morgan James Publishing. Morgan James and The Entrepreneurial Publisher are trademarks of Morgan James, LLC. www.MorganJamesPublishing.com

The Morgan James Speakers Group can bring authors to your live event. For more information or to book an event visit The Morgan James Speakers Group at www.TheMorganJamesSpeakersGroup.com.

BitLit
FOR ALL THE BOOKS YOU OWN

FREE eBook edition for your existing eReader with purchase

_____
PRINT NAME ABOVE

For more information, instructions, restrictions, and to register your copy, go to **www.bitlit.ca/readers/register** or use your QR Reader to scan the barcode:

ISBN 978-1-61448-946-7 paperback
ISBN 978-1-61448-947-4 eBook
ISBN 978-1-61448-949-8 HC/Dust Jacket
ISBN 978-1-63047-096-8 HC/Laminate
Library of Congress Control Number:
2013948911

Cover Design by:
Kathi Dunn
www.dunn-design.com

Interior Design by:
Bonnie Bushman
bonnie@caboodlegraphics.com

In an effort to support local communities, raise awareness and funds, Morgan James Publishing donates a percentage of all book sales for the life of each book to Habitat for Humanity Peninsula and Greater Williamsburg.

Get involved today, visit
www.MorganJamesBuilds.com

Habitat
for Humanity
Peninsula and
Greater Williamsburg
Building Partner

To my children,
that they will continue the tradition of giving first,
and be open to receive the
abundance that life has to offer.

To the spirit that guides me,
in gratitude and honor,
I give back this book.

Other Books, Products, and Programs

by Penny Tremblay

Workplace Relationships: Build positive, productive, and profitable relationships with strategies to improve communication and customer relations. This professional development program is delivered internationally in seminar, workshop, and keynote format.

Speak With Confidence—Deliver Powerful, Productive, and Profitable Presentations: This program is a must for anyone who wants to present with more impact, create lasting impressions, and call people to action, all of which will result in increased sales or a measurable difference in performance.

The Greatest You: Uncover your unique talents, experience your greatness, and begin a life filled with happiness and success as you apply ten principles toward becoming your personal best. This personal development program is delivered in seminar, workshop, keynote, or webinar format and is supported with a DVD, two-CD audio set, and eighty-eight-page workbook.

Work/Life Balance: Acquire meaningful daily achievement and enjoyment in the roles you deem important for yourself. Define balance and build awareness of where you are, what you want, and how to achieve and enjoy more in your personal and professional life. Delivered in seminar, workshop, or keynote format and supported with a CD audio program.

You're My Hero™ **by Barry Spilchuk and Penny Tremblay:** The power of praise, recognition, and acknowledgment is demonstrated time and time again in this 272-page anthology that recognizes everyday heroes.

Monthly Leadership Tips by Penny Tremblay, Director of the Tremblay Leadership Center: Bring leadership to the forefront in workplaces, families, and educational institutions internationally. Subscribe to your monthly copy and share it with friends. More than one hundred articles since 2004.

Visit **www.PennyTremblay.com** for all products.

Contents

Acknowledgments

Behind every great book is a team of influential people and supporters.

I am eternally grateful to my mom, Peggy Tremblay, who loves and supports me unconditionally, and to my dad, Richard Tremblay, now in spirit, who constantly guides me to be courageous.

The spiritual guidance I receive from God and Monsignor Dave Tramontini of the Pro Cathedral helps me to remain grounded, but also to reach upward to stretch my abilities and wisdom daily.

The icing on the cake of this project was meeting and working alongside the incredible Barbara De Angelis, whose support and mentorship offered a steady and stable guiding light on my journey. I have never been brighter, lighter, deeper, or more capable of serving the world than I have been since committing myself to transformation and self-mastery under her loving direction.

Special thanks to Kody Bateman, the founder and CEO of SendOutCards, for accepting my invitation to write this book's foreword. The mission of his company is closely related to my message: giving, celebrating people, receiving and earning, all in order to continue the circle of abundance in our lives. His leadership and achievements make him such a relevant contributor and inspiration to my work. Thanks also to Jordan Adler for taking the time to read some of my stories and interviews, and for his encouraging words about my skills that helped me soar like an eagle throughout this project. Thanks also to Leann McFalls, Emerald Moon, and Megan Drescher for paving my way to their executives, and to Melody Marler Forshee for her editing suggestions which helped me achieve a better end result.

Receiving the relentless support of Hobie Hobart and Kathi Dunn of Dunn+Associates Design has been an enormous blessing. Their cover design is simply brilliant, yet the light they shone for me was far beyond design, and pulled me forward from the moment I met Hobie early in this project.

Thank you to Rick and Scott Frishman, David Hancock, Margo Toulouse, Bethany Marshall, Jim Howard and the staff at Morgan James for believing in my vision and publishing *Give and Be Rich*. The interior layout and design by Bonnie Bushman gave these words a beautiful and permanent place in the world. I feel that the project is in masterful hands under your guidance and with your capable staff.

Thank you to my interviewees: Alison McGraw, Allie Braswell, Andrew Patricio, Arnya Assance, Barry Spilchuk, Christine Fortin, Crystal Kauffman, David Lamothe, David Perruzza, Dave and Lori Smith, Dennis Marangos, Eric Jackson, Gail Clark, Graham Robinson, Hariett Madigen, Jordan Adler, Jose Morales, Karen Brown, Kendra Neil, Kody Bateman, Laurie Hayes, Lisa Beedie-Verkuyl, Mario Lemay, Mary Jean Schmunk, Maurice Switzer, Michael Lewellen, Nick Lamatrice, Raquel Sticklee, Rick Frishman, Robert MacPhee, Robin Schleien, Saul Colt, Scott Clark, Sharon McQueen, Stan Cox, Steve Braybrook, Susan Hyatt, Suzanne Harmony, and Vanessa Brown. You helped bring this material to life. Your generous stories and examples will help millions of people understand and apply the concept of giving and being rich.

My professional connections have lifted me to heights that I could not have accomplished on my own. Thanks to Barry Spilchuk, Kevin Best, John Mitrano, Randy Peyser, and Angela Brown for editing assistance. Thanks also to Debbie Tremblay, Micheline Paquette, Laurie Hayes, Barry Spilchuk, Joshua Darnell, Monica Martin, David Lamothe and Tom Palangio for each reading at least one chapter before the book's final submission.

Gratitude is felt very deeply for those who encouraged me to continue writing—specifically Paul Barton, for inspiring me to write regularly after reading my first article, and Barry Spilchuk, who invited me to co-author the first *You're My Hero* book, which taught me a deeper lesson in giving. We were able to give the book's proceeds to charity and I became hooked on giving, and have firm intentions to raise charity dollars with this book as well. Not only has Barry been a great mentor and supporter of my dreams, he has become a dear friend.

I am so grateful for my monthly articles' readership, which has grown to many thousands. Your appreciation and feedback were the wind beneath my wings to build an inventory of what is now the foundation of my writing and speaking empire.

My virtual presence on the web would not be as dynamic if it were not for my developer and artist, Jon Valade, and my gifted and generous videographer, Kyle Selle.

Thanks to my coaches Jane Atkinson, for her concepts of being a wealthy speaker; Sam Horn, for intriguing me; Ron Hetherington, for technical word processing; and Tony Armstrong, Vanessa Brown, and Dr. William Johnston for my physical and emotional strength and alignment.

I have received so much support from my assistants Samantha Rodriguez and Emerson Stillar, who efficiently took care of business behind the scenes so I could focus on speaking, teaching and writing.

To all of my dear friends, family and healers, who continuously communicate their belief in me, act as my biggest fans, and constantly pick me up through challenging times—I wouldn't be who I am today without your confidence and belief in me. To Art and Debbie Tremblay, Brian and Nicki Dreger, Greg Beckham, June Williamson, Karen and Kelly Sarlo, Laurie Hayes, Mike Dagostino, Mitch and Jilles Paquette, Monica Martin, Nancy Anello, Sharon Armstrong, Shelley Hoffman, Susan Sequin and so many others... you are my rocks!

My support system at home is critical in preserving my ability to write and give so much of myself to others. I am eternally grateful to my partner David Neil, and to our long-time nanny Hazel Dones, for their endless support and contributions to our family.

To my son Ryan, for demonstrating consistency, determination and laser focus to his golf game which has inspired me with the same qualities for my work, and finally, a huge thank-you goes to my biggest cheerleader—my daughter Sierra—who asks me often, "How many pages did you write today, Mom? Who did you interview today, Mom?" It feels wonderful to receive back the support you've given all along.

Foreword

By Kody Bateman

I first met Penny Tremblay at one of my personal development seminars. She came up to me after the event with tears in her eyes and expressed her genuine connection with my "give for the sake of giving" philosophy. I instantly connected with what I like to call "the passion of Penny." When you meet her, or simply read the words of this book, you will know what I mean. She has a passion for the same "give to give" philosophy. She has an in-depth understanding of fundamental "Law of Attraction" principles. She instinctively knows, "What you send out in life is what you get back."

So many people give without expectation of any return. But these same people often find it hard to receive. Some believe they are not worthy, while others simply don't take the time to receive. In my book Promptings®, I share a story from my wife Jodi. At a salon one day, Jodi watched a daughter who was obviously a caregiver for an ailing mother, who came into the salon on oxygen. Both the mother and daughter sat down to get pedicures. The mother was clearly so grateful to her daughter as she finally relaxed and allowed herself to be pampered and taken care of. The daughter was clearly a nurturer. As Jodi watched, she realized it may be a stretch for the young daughter to pay for both pedicures. Acting on a prompting, Jodi paid their bill and asked for it to remain anonymous. As she enjoyed her own pedicure, Jodi watched as the salon owner told the daughter and mother that their bill had already been paid. The daughter could not believe it—she could not imagine anyone would do this for them! It was hard for this daughter to receive an act of kindness because she was so busy giving acts of kindness.

This is what many people get caught up in for most of their lives. Through the stories and examples in Penny's book, you will learn how to give and also leave yourself open to receive blessings and abundance—to achieve balance in your life. When people are in balance, they believe everyone is on equal ground and deserving. They know what they stand for. People who send this out receive emotions of acceptance, confidence, and love. What you send out is what you attract back.

My guiding principle for the past several years has been this: We all have goals to accomplish. We all have dreams to live. We all have a destiny to pursue. There are things in this world that only we can do. There are people in our lives that only we can touch or help at certain times. We must learn to manifest and receive the noble desires of our heart so we can share who we really are with the world.

Life is not about the destination. It's about the journey. It's about the stories you collect along the way. Being open to both giving and receiving will bring incredible stories throughout your life. As you read this book, I encourage you to journal the instances in which you can give as well as receive. And as you put "receiving" into practice in your life, your abundance will grow and your relationships with others will become stronger, healthier, and more productive. You will learn to love and help others, share blessings, and let your capacity for greatness shine as you open your life to both give and receive.

Penny Tremblay has put together a remarkable collection of time-tested principles and sprinkled the "passion of Penny" on them. I am honored to call her my friend and I am better prepared for ongoing prosperity after reading this book.

Kody Bateman
Founder & CEO, SendOutCards
Best-selling author of Promptings®:
Your Inner Guide to Making a Difference

Introduction

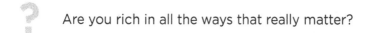

"If you consistently give, you will consistently have."
—Fortune Cookie

Are you rich in all the ways that really matter?

When we think of growing rich, money comes to mind, but life has so many currencies. Money is one of them. Good relationships, health, time, mobility, high self-esteem, and deeper spirituality are a few others. It is human nature to want more—more money, more time, more love, more energy, more success. We all possess an inner drive to have more, achieve more, and create a more fulfilling life. The good news is that **we can have whatever we want when we learn to circulate abundance.**

The circle of abundance is equally about giving and receiving. Circulating abundance starts with giving. Giving starts the receiving process and comes before receiving, in the dictionary and in life. We can have everything we desire in terms of happy relationships, vitality, professional success, and financial wealth if we give enough people what they want and need. When we give what we have in order to benefit others, we receive in like kind or greater—that is, if we allow ourselves to receive the bounty that life offers.

The paradox of giving yet having more is explained in this book. You will learn how you can attain personal and business growth through giving—first to yourself, then to others and charitable organizations, as well as in business. You also will learn why receiving is equally as important.

Blocking the Flow

Do you feel like you need to hold on tight, with a closed fist, to what you have for fear of not having enough? The money you've worked for, the possessions you own, your time, your freedom, your happiness? Therein lies the problem. When we hold on to energy of any type, it creates a blockage.

Imagine your arm with a closed fist. It has one channel to give and receive. Now open your hand and extend all fingers as wide as you can. You now have five channels from which you can both give and receive. Opening up to give more increases the flow back to you.

You can't put anything into a closed fist, which means you have to be open to receive and in order to give. If you are resistant to receiving, your circulation of abundance is cut off, and over time you'll have little or nothing to give.

We lack the ability to feel worthy and deserving of life's abundance when we are not willing to receive. Likewise, when we do not give, we suffocate the flow of good fortune that can come to us, because we are holding back. It is law.

The concept of *Give and Be Rich* is that we must first look within and give of ourselves, with no expected return. When a return does come knocking, however, we must open the door to receive the flow inward.

For example, many people grow up with an entitlement attitude; they believe the world owes them something. They have one channel, and they use it for taking. Others feel they aren't worthy or deserving of abounding wealth, so they use their one or many channels to give, yet they close themselves off to receiving. Can you see a blockage in both cases? When we open ourselves to the flow of abundance, we can create the life we desire and deserve.

The Riches of an Abundant Mind

The essence of our being is to love and be happy, but the value that society has placed on money and material things has caused much grief and dissatisfaction. Too often we feel that we are lacking or limited in some way because we cannot buy the material goods we see advertised or see other people enjoying. On the other hand, those who can buy any or all of the material things they want aren't necessarily buying happiness. Once the novelty of owning the items wears off, they realize that owning more stuff doesn't help them maintain happiness and inner peace.

We lack satisfaction when we focus on external material things. Objects cannot nurture our deepest desires of what really matters to us. Due to this inability to connect with our desires, we turn to other stimulants. We numb our unhappiness with excessive busy-ness, or the use of drugs, alcohol, sex, food, and material things such as shopping—all to chase a feeling or a high that *already lives inside us* and just needs to be nurtured. Living life to chase more money or material things does not give us the feeling of peace and contentment we think it would. But giving and receiving does.

Many people don't think they have anything to give and live lives of financial desperation because they are so focused on money. Money determines their self-value. Money, however, is merely paper and ink. It's the value we place on money that gives it its worth.

What if we valued people, relationships, our customers, our time, our talents, our feelings and our spiritual selves just as much as we value money? We would realize we are already rich in many ways. The benefit of feeling rich in many ways is that we attract more of what we think and feel. We open up to being prosperous. Rather than loving things, and using people, we grow rich by loving people and using things. Luxury is wonderful, and material things are terrific, and we deserve all of the lavishness that life has to offer. Loving people *and* enjoying extravagance—doesn't that sound amazing?

Receiving the Gifts in This Book

The source of creating and circulating abundant wealth is the Spirit. This book will nurture the spiritual source within you. You'll have many questions to ask yourself after reading examples and stories that will bring context to this information as it applies to your life.

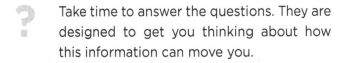

Take time to answer the questions. They are designed to get you thinking about how this information can move you.

Journal the answers that come to you, and take action on the valuable opportunities to *give* the appropriate change or shift a chance to *grow* by capturing your thoughts on paper and reviewing them until they manifest into your desired actions and behaviors. Several pages of journaling space have been provided at the back of the book.

With the examples and strategies offered in this book, you can put your stake in the ground and gain tremendous momentum toward what you want by leveraging your thoughts, actions, and time. You can let go of the need to hoard things and also give away what you already have to begin the dynamic exchange of circulating the flow of abundant energy in your life.

Sometimes giving means learning to say no or letting go of things or beliefs or circumstances, both past or present, and even letting go of people who no longer serve our highest and best interests.

If you think you have nothing to give, are bored, unhappy, depressed, disappointed, heartbroken, lonely, rich, happy, healthy or full of joy, this book will be an inspiration for you. If you already are a super-duper giver, this book will show you how you can receive abundantly.

My profession places a large emphasis on leadership. When people ask what I do, I tell them I'm a teacher, because my career is rooted in being a servant leader; in sharing, teaching, and encouraging others to succeed; and in inspiring them to wish, hope, dream, and then make it happen.

It takes work and effort to walk to the talk in this book, but the payoff is grand. It's easier for me to teach ten seminars, do ten keynotes, or write ten books on this subject than it is to really *live* all the lessons contained within, but I work on polishing these concepts as I experience life every day. On my quest for greatness and riches, I read, write, and am constantly reminded of the lessons I need to learn, implement, and master in my own life. My desire to share fuels my motivation to write so that my messages can reach the masses. From giving my written and spoken words to elevate others, I have amassed a following of thousands of people and look forward to serving millions in my lifetime.

If there is one thing that helps propel me to success, it is the way I feel, and feelings do fluctuate.

Thoughts and Feelings Are the Ticket to Success

When we feel good, we attract good things. Thoughts become things. To "think and grow rich," as taught by Napoleon Hill, is vital, because our thoughts begin the process of our results. Feelings, however, are a major part of the formula too. **Feeling rich and abundant will catapult you toward attracting the life you want.** Ultimately, the life you think and feel becomes the life you live.

> The question all individuals, families, business owners, employees, citizens, or any human being needs answered is "How can I feel good every day, despite any circumstance?" The answer is by giving and allowing yourself to receive.

After giving to yourself as a foundation for creating greatness, you can harness the strengths of other people by investing in them and celebrating them. We all possess the ability to reach out and give to others, regardless of whether our gift is money, material items, service, words of encouragement, a greeting card, a smile, a prayer, or a compliment. Giving to others gives us a great sense of joy, and joy is the highest feeling on the scale of emotions. Abundant wealth, therefore, is within your reach and begins with remembering who you are at your core, identifying with your desires and intentions, and then giving yourself to others in service.

True success isn't earned at the expense of others by taking from them, but by first giving to people. The ticket to creating abundantly therefore is found in feeling good about the relationship we have with ourselves and others.

Learn Many Ways to Give and Receive

Throughout this book, I explore the concepts of giving and receiving and why they are critical to the circulation of wealth and abundance. As the riches of life are not only monetary, I explore many other valuable assets that leave us feeling joy and ultimately assist us in attracting all riches into our lives.

There are two sides to abundance. One is giving, and the other equally important one is receiving. When you're a great giver, you'll feel worthy and deserving of receiving. This is a cycle of enthusiasm, which you can tap into no matter what age or stage you are at in your life.

This book provides information and activities to help you recognize your deepest desires and identify what you already have to give in order to receive. These important blueprints for success are a fundamental step in the process of personal planning. Once we have the foundation of awareness, we are clear on what to do, what to give ourselves, and how to interact effectively and productively with the people in our lives.

If the key to riches lies in the relationships we create and maintain with people, and people are beings of emotion, motivated by pride and self-importance, then even the gift of a smile, prayer, or positive thought directed at someone can make a significant impact. Tap into the idea of giving people what *they* want and create exceptional relationships.

In business, we get started to satisfy a customer need yet often lose focus on the customer as we strive for profit. Recognizing the importance of maintaining client relationships will set you apart from the competition. The numerous valuable strategies and real-life examples in this book will ensure that your business remains first in the minds of customers and prospects, and first in their choice when deciding who will supply their needs. People do business with those they know, like, and trust. Relationships mean everything, so appreciating others always wins over promoting one's business or self. Recognizing others does not have to cost money or take a lot of time; make a phone call, send a card or handwritten note, or speak words of genuine gratitude.

Our own communities could not function without the assistance of volunteers and financial contributions. Likewise, volunteers could not function with the same self-worth if they were not giving of themselves. People grow rich by giving.

No matter who or where you are in your life when you read this, you have what it takes to give and receive tremendous value. It's time to change your mindset from needing to have and holding on to what you have - to one of wanting to give, share, serve, make an investment in yourself and others, and receive abundantly.

This book will help you unlock the belief that you must have money already to find deeper success.

Throughout my life, I have witnessed *giving* as the most efficient way to build and maintain relationships with people and to advance my career. Since the age of eleven, I've been employed in service-oriented sales businesses, and I've spent years developing and honing my communication skills to bridge relations with people so they feel cared about. I have also done the opposite, and made mistakes in life and in business, putting ego before love or profits before customer service. This did not serve me well, and I have learned many lessons.

Growing up as the youngest child, with two older brothers and loving parents in a middle-class family in Sudbury, Ontario, Canada, I moved into my teen years with a conscious awareness of a message from my soul—**that gratitude and offering service to others was the way for me to find joy, self-worth, esteem, and happiness**.

Our family owned a seasonal campground business as a source of sideline income. I was only eleven years old when we took possession of the campground, but I still recall the celebration dinner at Marconi's steakhouse. Our family began the new chapter of our lives by clinking our glasses together in a toast to honor our financial ability to acquire this new property. I vividly remember my father telling us children that he and my mother had remortgaged our house to purchase the campground and that if anything happened that we lost the business property, we would lose our home as well.

"We need your hard work and your contribution to make this business successful," explained my father. Gulp! The steak didn't go down so easy that night, knowing the realities of taking a business risk, but the thought of having the ability to make a difference with my efforts engaged me to want to make this family business work. As teenagers, we gave that business a great deal of effort. My parents worked at their full-time jobs, as well as at this part-time seasonal business, and as a family, we became rich in the end. The end came seventeen years later, when my parents sold the campground to their successors. The business had grown from nine to 117 seasonal campers. We had built a family business that had given other families an opportunity to enjoy their summers. We became rich with new friendships; rich with a wealth of skills learned in the areas of customer service, teamwork, and overcoming challenges; and rich with the lesson of the value of giving to others.

Through giving to others, I continue to create and circulate abundant wealth every day. In my daily reflection, I ask God to help me achieve my purpose of helping millions of people achieve their goals. He sent me the title for this book and the guidance for its content.

My wish for you is that you fully understand the value in giving to others and that you receive the self-gratitude gained by loving yourself unconditionally and giving yourself away in service.

As the lessons learned by giving seem to point to the greatest answer for leading a happy life, I wanted to write a book about the concept to share experiences and stories with more people than my speaking, training, and written material could extend to.

I believe our planet is in a time of rebirth. As we enter a new age, our human race is awakening and evolving toward a higher consciousness. We are being called from self-centered living to spirit-centered, co-creative, people-centered consciousness. I feel a sense of urgency to help people tap into their passion, vision, intention, and clarity about what they have to give and why they deserve to receive in the circle of abundance.

In my effort to help raise the world's vibration toward serving and helping one another, my intention is to influence millions more people to look within, value their gifts, share, care, and co-create a world in which we can all enjoy life's riches.

How Do We Grow Rich?

You can have wealth, and you deserve all the wealth and abundance that you can imagine. The key is to release your attachment to wealth and money and give your best to share and serve humanity. The riches will come—that is, if you **allow** them in. Are you ready to enrich the lives of others and reap the benefits?

I interviewed many people who were attracted to this project because they are great givers. Their contribution of stories and examples about how giving to others has enhanced their personal lives and careers will inspire you. In their stories, my own experiences, and some folklore and anecdotes, you will experience the law of prosperity, the law of attraction, and the law of giving from ordinary people and highly successful people.

All of them share one thing in common—they started giving, opened up to receiving, and have tapped the circle of abundance.

A frequent question emerged while I interviewed the greatest givers: "Can you teach me how to receive?" Within this question lies an important key to wealth. People are challenged in regard to both giving and receiving.

The chapters that lie ahead are ordered for your success. Let's get started.

> *"No one can become rich without enriching others.*
> *Anyone who adds to prosperity must prosper in turn."*
> **—G. Alexander Orndorff**

 **CHAPTER 1**

Giving Simply to Give

"Even after all this time,
the sun never says to the earth 'you owe me.' "
—Hafiz

*W*hen we give, we instantly grow rich—rich in the feeling of having done something for someone else. This feeling is the spark that propels the circle of abundance.

Would you like to get more out of life?
Would you like to get more out of your relationships?
Would you like to get more love?
Would you like to get more money?
Would you like to get more sales?
Would you like to get more stuff?

There's a simple way to get all of these things and anything else. Read the following statement aloud: "Getting Is Very Easy!" Now look at the first letter of each word: G-I-V-E. The key to getting whatever you want is to first G-I-V-E.

Giving can be defined as making a contribution, and the net effect of contributing is that we are richer for it.

You may be asking, "How can I give what I don't have?" You innately already have what you want and need. You only need to believe and have faith. Therefore, whatever you desire in your life, you can give away to others. It may be available for you to give on a smaller scale, and to receive on a larger scale, but giving will start the receiving process in the circle of abundance.

What can you contribute or give away that you already have? Well… everything and anything good! This list below will vary with each person, but it's a good start:

Love	*Listening*
Service	*Encouragement*
Time	*Commitment*
Patience	*Hope*
Space	*Confidence*
Talent	*Appreciation*
Prayer	*A smile*
Positive thoughts	*Knowledge*
Good intentions	*Opportunity*
Persistence	*Money*
Determination	*Acceptance*
Interest	*Compliments*
Understanding	*And much more*

"Wouldn't it be nice to live in a world where we can
Love for the sake of Loving, Share for the sake of
Sharing, and Give for the sake of Giving?"
—Mark Victor Hansen

Unconditional Giving

Giving *unconditionally* is key. If we simply give without the expectation of receiving anything in return, we are giving properly. Many people, however give with conditions attached. They have an underlying motivation for giving; one common motivation is recognition, another is control. This is our ego working, wanting to be right, wanting to be noticed, wanting to protect us from being vulnerable. I believe that the hearts that give—in any capacity and without any expectation of return or favor—will be the most richly blessed. Furthermore, when we give in secrecy or anonymity, we receive in greater abundance. Give without the expectation of receiving anything in return. When you give with the intention of getting something back, you just don't make the same impact.

I'd like to share a story about intention and desire that grew tall with deep roots in giving.

"It's been remarkable to sit back and think about all of the wonderful experiences where I have given and received in life." This was the first comment Laurie made in our interview about the "Give and Be Rich" concept. She went on to tell me a story about something someone gave her that still has an impact on her life.

One day while working in a 911 call dispatch job, she casually said to her coworker, Lenore, "I want an oak tree. I love oak trees, and I have many other types of trees around me, but no oak trees."

The following Monday, Lenore came into the office smiling. "I was hiking with my husband on the weekend," she told Laurie, "and I brought you back your oak tree." She held out a closed fist and said, "Here's your oak tree," and she dropped an acorn into Laurie's hand.

Laurie and her friend laughed together. "In a 911 dispatch center, you have to lighten the mood often, so we were accustomed to silliness and fun in the workplace," Laurie says.

Laurie, however, took the little oak seed seriously. She brought it home, planted it in soil, and tended to it, fully expecting it to manifest into her much wanted big and bold tree.

Eventually the tree sprouted. When the tree was about four inches tall, Laurie planted her in the yard of a home where she was staying temporarily. When she moved into her next home within a year, she dug up the small tree and planted it again in what is now the tree's permanent residence. Laurie named the tree Lenore, after her colleague, who saw potential in the seed and her desire.

"My workplace colleague passed away a few years later," Laurie says, "but her legacy lives on in my front yard. Lenore listened to what I had to say in a random conversation about wanting an oak tree. She proved her thoughtfulness by taking action and gave of herself to connect me and my tree. Her giving had nothing to do with money, but everything to do with taking action on something special for someone else."

Lenore now has a thirty-foot-tall legacy growing in her honor. Her memory will live on for the next hundred years or more.

> *"Your imagination is your preview of life's coming attractions."*
> **—Albert Einstein**

The Law of Giving

In every acorn is the promise of a thousand forests, provided that it is planted in fertile ground. Seeds are not meant to be hoarded. They must be sown, and so it is with our gifts that we have to give to others. They too must be sown.

Our bodies, our minds, and the universe all operate through a constant dynamic exchange of energy, which is comprised of giving and receiving. To stop this circulation of energy would be like stopping the flow of blood in our bodies. We would stagnate, rot, and die. We must consistently give and receive to maintain the flow of wealth and affluence in our lives.

The Law of Attraction

Rooted in metaphysics, the law of attraction states that your thoughts, the images in your mind, and the feelings connected to them later manifest as your reality. In other words, all that exists in your life right now, whether positive or negative, has been attracted to you through your mind. You can attract whatever you want into your life. That's a universal law, just like the law of gravity. We cannot see the effects of the law of attraction as quickly or clearly as the law of gravity—gravity immediately pulls a loose object toward the floor—yet the law of attraction brings you exactly what you are thinking about and exactly what you are feeling.

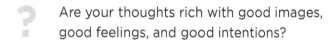

Are your thoughts rich with good images, good feelings, and good intentions?

Herein lies the importance of giving to yourself first, as a foundation for all prosperity to ebb and flow in your life. A fully open channel is contagious and attracts fully open opportunities to give and receive. The vibration of giving opens the channel wider and wider, and allows the incoming energy to fill you more and more. Paying attention to how abundance vibrates within you and making proper corrections is a worthwhile investment of your time and energy. I explore the concept of giving to yourself in Chapter 3.

Like Attracts Like

We get what we give. We reap what we sow. When we help others, we receive feelings of pride and fulfillment, which we also wish for the people we help. This is why constantly looking for ways to give to people every day is so valuable. It makes them feel precious, and we reap the benefits too; it's a win/win situation.

The key to attracting riches is to give without expecting results. In other words, don't pay tribute to someone with a hidden agenda—

for example, getting them to like you or gaining for yourself in some way, such as a receiving a promotion, a raise, or an increase in popularity. If you do give with expectation, you will attract back to you exactly that—a tribute paid back to you with a hidden agenda or an expectation.

Instead, offer to help when and where you can in love and service to others. This is practicing **altruism**. You will feel rich just for giving, period. In time, you will experience abundance returned to you. By then you'll be doubly blessed. How will you feel when someone shares their time and service with you just because you deserve it?

> *"We all receive according to how much we give.*
> *Give the best of you everywhere you go.*
> *Give a smile. Give thanks. Give kindness. Give love."*
> —**Rhonda Byrne**, *The Secret*

The Riches of Life

Are you rich in all the ways that really matter? The secret to riches exists in the relationships we keep—the relationships we have with ourselves, and with others, in our personal and professional lives.

I asked Jordan Adler, the top income earner in his network marketing company, "What is the greatest richness that you experience in your life?"

"I usually get asked why I keep doing the business when I am in a group of people," he replied. "My answer is just that—the ability to share experiences and share dreams with my friends all over the world. That's what I love to do. That's what drives me. That's what gets me really excited about life— to experience really fun places and have my friends with me. People did that for me when I was just getting started. Before I had the financial resources to do those things, I was invited to fly on private jets and stay in castles in Scotland and have dinner on the Fenn in Europe. They helped me stretch my dreams. I consider myself somewhat of a dream broker."

I followed up my first question with a second question, "Why do you feel you've been invited to experience these luxuries?"

"To get invited into the inside circle," Jordan said, "I had to demonstrate integrity and my desire to learn. I had to demonstrate my decision by taking initiative, showing gratitude to the people who had contributed to my life, investing in myself through professional development, and investing in others."

"If I understand you correctly, you had to first give to grow rich," I said.

"Yes. I invested a lot in myself and others to grow to where I am today."

There is great value in discovering your gifts, and giving them away.

"The only gift is a portion of thyself."
—Ralph Waldo Emerson

"Checks" Aren't Always Monetary

Alison was devastated when her husband left her for another woman at Christmas. His only gift to her was their $52,000 debt. Even though he had walked away, Alison was accountable for the entire amount, yet the money she was bringing in from her salary wasn't sufficient to cover the debt and support herself at the same time. She had to make a decision that would affect her for years; she had to declare personal bankruptcy.

Alison spent her days feeling extremely sorry for herself, until one quick decision changed her life forever. She met a person who was planning to donate their time at a local soup kitchen on Christmas day.

I'm alone. I have nothing else to do, she thought. I can also give my time to help others."

"This was a pivotal moment in my life," Alison says. "In giving away my time to help those who were less fortunate, I realized how rich I really was—rich in time to give, rich in health with which to serve others, and rich with a future to continue to make a difference."

With her new part-time Mary Kay business, Alison started giving back by sharing her time with others and teaching them about skin care to help them feel beautiful. She's also opened her eyes to different opportunities to give, such as visiting cancer patients in their homes to pamper them and make their day.

"It makes me feel confident to be giving and making a difference in other people's lives," says Alison. "From that new feeling of being useful, needed, and abundant, I began to shift out of the mindset of being a victim of someone else's decision and into a mindset of giving service to others, which has helped me love myself more."

In no time, the floodgates opened up in Alison's life. People wanted to work with her. She was asked to help on special projects and was recognized as one of the "Top 40 People Under 40" by the North Bay Chamber of Commerce. "This all came to me because I was giving my time to help people in the community who were worse off than I was," she says.

Alison changed her mindset to believe that being left by her husband and facing financial challenges were opportunities to learn what really made her feel kind-hearted. Giving back to the community and giving to people in general gave her a feeling of true richness. When she acted from her heart instead of her ego, opportunity and prosperity poured into her life.

"This check was not monetary, like most are," Alison explains. "This was a reality check that earned me an enormous amount of joy, esteem, and desire to go on doing the right things."

Get What You Give

There is an old notion that 'what goes around comes around' meaning that whatever you want to attract into your life must first be given away. Even a thought about what you want is a start. It's something you generate and give away.

For example, if we want and need to feel love and belongingness, we need to think thoughts of love and belongingness about ourselves and others. We shouldn't dwell on our lack of these things but think actual thoughts about how it feels to love, to be loved, and to belong. Furthermore, we must actually *feel* these experiences. If you want to feel needed, you must give yourself away. In giving yourself away, you will instantly feel needed. If you want more compliments, you must give away compliments. You will feel thoughtful in complimenting others. If you want more money, you must give money away. If you want more love in your life, you must give love away.

> **?** Are you too busy listening to the radio station WII-FM, (What's in it for Me) to give to others?

You can give yourself the feeling of satisfying your needs simply by fulfilling someone else. Try giving to people just for the sake of giving, and watch what happens. When you give from the heart, the return is tenfold, and that reality check is worth a mint.

> *"Remember, you cannot receive what you don't give.*
> *Outflow determines inflow."*
> —Eckhart Tolle

The Power of Precise Intentions

Several years ago our family had the unfortunate and heartbreaking experience of unexpectedly losing a family member near and dear to our hearts. My parents are "snowbirds," which means that as Canadians they vacation for a long time in the southern part of Florida during the winter months. In March of 2009, we visited them for a fun-filled week with our children. The day we left, we received a phone call and learned that my father had suffered a severe stroke and was undergoing emergency surgery.

The end of my father's life was a sudden reality that hit us like a ton of bricks. Friends, support, and sympathy poured into their Florida home over the next few days while we solemnly packed my parents' possessions in preparation for my father's funeral in Canada. Although my mother received many loving invitations to return to the Florida community of Water Oaks in Lady Lake the following winter, she couldn't bear the thought of returning to the home that held the memories of the tragic ending of her loving husband's life.

Before we left for Canada, we listed their home with a local real estate agent. A "for sale" sign went up, and it was one of many on the street. In 2008, the US mortgage crisis had created a frenzy of troubles for many homeowners. My parents' Florida home sat between two others for sale and across the street from two more. This pattern repeated itself along the street and throughout the entire community. Several months passed without anyone showing interest in my parents' property.

I had just finished reading *Excuse Me, Your Life is Waiting* by Lynn Grabhorn, a book about the importance of using feelings when you intend to create something in your life. My mother and I decided to create the sale of the home in our minds and hearts. We visualized the process step by step until the deal closed and Mom did a happy dance. We included every detail: the sounds, the words, the actions, and the feelings.

Our creation went exactly like this: The phone would ring, and a cheerful voice on the other end would say, "Hello, Peggy! This is Buffy from the Water Oak Country Club realtor's office. We have an offer on your home, and it's a solid offer. Can I fax it over?"

Of course, my mother had the fax number of a local community center in her area that she had found in advance with the expectation of needing it. When the realtor called, she would provide the number, jump into her van, and drive over to the community center to collect her fax.

The offer would be a sound offer—almost her asking price. The new inhabitants would be a fun-loving couple, just like my parents, who would enjoy the home and the community life of the Country Club. My mom would accept the offer and fax back the documents. She would drive home and enter her living room, feeling relieved and free for having just sold her property. She would feel these feelings, feel gratitude toward the real estate agent, and feel excited to look for a new home in the same area. She would feel herself moving to the beat of her happy dance.

In our minds, we played out this visualization every day for about a month.

One day while visiting her, my mother told me there hadn't yet been any action on the property and that she hadn't heard from her agent. As my mother was taking a trip to Las Vegas, we sent her agent a greeting card to communicate our appreciation for her and to advise her of a change in contact persons should any action take place while my mother was vacationing. The greeting card was simple. It contained a verse that read, "In this card I must include my sincere and heartfelt gratitude." We personalized the card further: "Buffy, I appreciate your showing the house and working to find a new homeowner to enjoy it as much as we had. Should there be any action requiring my signature between Sept. 20 and Oct. 9, please contact my daughter, Penny, at this number. Thanks again for all you are doing! Signed, Peggy Tremblay."

On October 1, I received the call.

"Hello, Penny? This is Buffy from the Water Oak Country Club. Your mother wrote me and said to call you if there was an offer. We have an offer on the home, and it's a solid offer. I think your mom would accept it. Where can I fax it?"

The rest, of course, is history. I tracked down my mother in Las Vegas and sent her the paperwork to sign and return, and it was with her tour group that she did her happy dance.

I never doubted that this process of setting intentions and creating a process in our minds with vivid visualizations, facts, and feelings would play out, but I was really blown away by its accuracy, speed, and effectiveness, so I called Buffy to inquire about the new buyers and how it all had happened, just to be nosy and to satisfy my own curiosity.

The realtor told me the couple was from New York. They saw the listing online and drove all the way to Florida to look at the house. When they entered the house, they felt wonderful, warm energy that made them want to stay. The lady had said, "I feel so welcome here. I just wish I could stay here." The agent had replied, "You can! You just need to make an offer."

You just can't make this stuff up. It came to be through the power of intention and deliberate creation, and we can all tap into this potential.

In the real estate market of 2009, with my parents' home competing against hundreds and hundreds of others within a twenty-five-mile radius, we deliberately created this property sale for ourselves, by giving our thoughts and feelings specific direction and details toward the results we intended to create.

Good, Good, Good, Good Vibrations

Thinking is not quite enough to get you on the powerful frequency of attracting—but feeling is. If you want to attract something, you must deeply feel an appreciation or desire for it. Appreciation is the highest and fastest vibration that we use for attracting. Give appreciation!

Let's say you want to attract love into your life. You walk around feeling love for people, flowing loving energy to people, and shooting appreciation toward people. You will attract love.

Do you remember falling in love? The feeling of walking on air? Everything being beautiful, bright, warm, perfectly perfect, and euphoric? Feel that feeling of being in love, and you will attract love.

If we felt appreciation all day long, we'd end up with more friends, more money, more vivacious health, and a closer connection to our spiritual energy than we ever imagined possible.

Thoughts manifest to reality quicker when you include feelings. If you want superb things, you've got to vibrate out superb feelings. Appreciation can take you there faster than any other feeling. Feeling appreciation is a major key to tapping the circle of abundance. Get into the habit of feeling awesome. It's your choice, your right, and your responsibility. You are *response-able,* so respond with appreciation. Choose to feel appreciation! Praise yourself, praise others, and be grateful for all that is. Appreciate with no strings attached, no expectations and watch what happens.

The Power in Feeling Appreciation

We constantly send out energy on a certain frequency. There are three states of frequency. The first is a low vibration, a victim state, in which we feel as though everyone and everything is against us; we negatively attract back exactly what we are giving out. The second is a mediocre state, neither up nor down, not really attracting anything except others' energy because we're going with the flow of everyone else. The third is a high-frequency state of pure positive energy that flows outward and attracts positive events and circumstances toward us.

 What frequency do you want to be vibrating at?

It's your choice, your right, and—yes!—your decision. You most likely want to be tuned into the level of high-frequency positive energy, which is where appreciation plays a vital role. To inhabit this higher vibration anytime and anywhere, think thoughts and feel feelings of appreciation—for example, *I'm so happy and grateful that I can step back and think about this situation.*

The vibration of appreciation is the most profound for our higher selves, because it's in perfect harmony with our "source energy," our "God energy," or whatever spiritual name you give to our higher power, the Creator of all things. One minute of allowing this intense and appreciative energy to flow through you can override thousands of hours spent in states of feeling victimized or mediocre. We all have an inner guidance system connected to our source energy. This energy desires only love and abundance. All else creates collisions within. When we vibrate out love and abundance by seeing love and feeling love, guess what happens? Our vibration finds a matching vibration for us. At that point, we must be willing to receive.

Giving and receiving are equally important in the circle of abundance. The next chapter will guide you to become just as good at receiving as you are at giving.

> *"We make a living out of what we get,*
> *but we make a life by what we give."*
> **—Winston Churchill**

 **CHAPTER 2**

The Importance of Receiving

"Know that you deserve to receive good in all ways."
—**Doreen Virtue**

When tapping the circle of abundance, we give first, and then we receive. Both are equally important. Giving and receiving are like both sides of your hand; you can't have one without the other.

It's likely that you're reading this book because you want to receive more.

? Have you ever thought about how you receive? Have you considered what exists beyond money and materialism? Are you open to receiving? Do you ask for what you need and allow what comes? Do you observe the subtle messages or listen for answers? Do you feel worthy and deserving to receive? Just how much are you willing to receive? What are your barriers to receiving? Do you have an abundance mentality or a scarcity mentality?

Give yourself the time and attention you need to reflect and/or write in a journal about these important questions. If you're unsure how to uncover the truth about these questions and reflect on the solutions, simply read on, but come back to these questions; they're a process in themselves. This book will help you discover more about yourself and why you are worthy of receiving. These questions are the basis of the pages to come. Receive them.

First, Let's Define Riches

The riches of life are not measured only in money and materialism. Who on their deathbed wishes they had more money or more stuff? Real richness is experienced in our relationships with our self and others, in lasting friendships and harmonious family relationships, in sympathy and empathy for other people, in understanding and accepting one another, and in feeling an abundance of peace, unconditional love, freedom and divinity.

For his bestselling book *Think and Grow Rich*, Napoleon Hill surveyed people to determine a list of their prioritized riches. The results included a positive attitude, good health, harmonious relationships, freedom from fear, hope (achievement), faith (commitment), sharing, love, openness, self-discipline, wisdom, and financial security. Notice that money comes near the end of this list of surveyed priorities. Financial abundance is awesome, and most of us desire to be wealthy. Monetary wealth is a healthy part of the balance of the riches of life.

We can place wealth—or prosperity—into three categories of currencies.

Good feelings: the ability to love ourselves; to attain desirable physical, emotional, and spiritual health; to understand and empathize with others; and to feel gratified about who we are and the contributions we make.

Good relationships: lasting friendships; strong, harmonious family relationships; and lucrative business and professional relationships.

Good finances and wealth: an abundance of pleasing things and the ability to enjoy them, including time, mobility, money, assets, and other material things we desire.

True richness requires a balance of these three categories. Abundance is the fullness or wholeness of all of these things. It is an endless flowing loop of energy, which is inherent in the natural flow of life. Creating a relationship with abundant energy will bring a more natural flow, both inward and outward of all good things.

Open the Channels

To be a consummate giver, you must allow yourself to receive. "Crystal, why do you feel worthy and deserving of the abundant life you lead?" I once asked a successful entrepreneur whom I was mentoring. "Sometimes I think it's easier to think of the bad stuff than the wonderful stuff," she admitted, "but I try to keep my thoughts and feelings on positive things. My parents instilled good values in me—to be kind to people and to work hard. They taught me to be a giver of myself, in time or money, and this seems to have opened as many channels for receiving that were needed to give."

Only in her twenties, Crystal operates a successful BioPed franchise and balances it with a new family, including a toddler and a preschooler.

She already has received in many ways, including good values that her parents taught her and examples of strong work ethic. Shortly after she completed a two-year mentorship program with me, Crystal's business received the prestigious award of Best Business in Ontario from the Canadian Youth Business Foundation (CYBF), which connected the two of us together.

The CYBF asked me to donate an hour a week for two years to help this local, young entrepreneur. I agreed and served. Crystal was very open to receiving any information and assistance I could share. From what I've told you, you may think I was on the giving end, and Crystal on the receiving end of our mentorship arrangement. So did I when I contemplated taking on the responsibility. At the end of our two years together, however, I realized I had received much more than I had given. I'd received recognition in national newspapers, community recognition, referrals, and questions for which I had to research and investigate answers. In sum, I grew a lot.

While interviewing other masterful givers, I uncovered a common question: "Can you teach me how to receive as well as I give?" Many of the people I spoke to weren't as open to receiving as Crystal was.

———————— ◎ ————————

Receiving should be effortless, but many people have challenges with it. As long as you open to continuous receiving, there will never be depletion, therefore, the more you allow yourself to receive, the more you can give away.

Unwillingness to Receive

"Why are people not willing to receive?" This question came up time and again in my research for this book. People who are unwilling to receive could be attached to some limiting belief that they are not worthy, or they have fear and guilt surrounding abundance. A limiting belief is something we spend time and attention on that doesn't serve us. Some attachments might be concerns about what others think, our own opinions of wealthy people, or how we fear that becoming abundant may ruin our lives or jeopardize our safety or happiness. Because of these unconscious attachments to limiting beliefs, we prejudge ourselves. We set ourselves up for lack and limitation.

Receiving also can be daunting because people don't want to "owe" anyone back.

If we're not willing to receive all of the gifts that come our way, and uncover who we really are underneath all of our limiting beliefs, we limit our potential.

Refusal to Receive

I have a wonderful friend named Barry. I had admired him from a distance until I was able to meet him personally, and eventually I ended up moving across the street from him. (I would have previously said, "What a coincidence" but I now say, "How symbolic," because I believe we attract what we think about.)

Our friendship was based on the common denominator of public speaking. Barry was doing a lot more of it than I was, and I wanted to learn from him. He was the first Canadian co-author for Jack Canfield and Mark Victor Hansen's *Chicken Soup for the Soul* collection, and I too wanted to be a famous author one day.

Barry helped me every chance he had, and like a sponge, I absorbed everything he offered. He never asked for anything in return. I felt blessed. One day he asked me to co-author the first *You're My Hero*™ book with him. The project was structured to give all proceeds to charity. I accepted, and since then my life has never been the same. We sold more than 2,700 books and donated more than $27,000 to local charities in a two-month period. I became hooked on giving.

The law of giving is not complete without receiving.

One day, as Barry was leaving his therapist's office, he put his hand on the doorknob, turned to the man, and started to cry. "You know what it is?" he said. "I feel like I've been giving to the whole world my entire life, and I just want someone to give to and take care of me."

Four months later, Barry found himself in the Princess Margaret Hospital Cancer Program. He had gone from being a prominent member of his community, a Chicken Soup for the Soul author and an author of many other books, a motivational speaker and trainer, and president of the local chamber of commerce to a cancer patient incapable of taking care of himself.

"Along the lines of 'Be careful what you ask for,' inadvertently, this is exactly what I asked for," Barry says. "I wanted people to give to me and take care of me. So what I received was being reduced to an infantile level where I needed my most basic needs provided for."

One of the most important lessons Barry needed to learn was how to receive—how to let other people help him. "It all came from throwing my arms up in the air and saying 'I can't give anymore.' This was God's way of giving me what I needed more than anything, which was allowing others to give to me."

In the past, Barry had often asked for money for local nonprofits and fundraising events, but he couldn't ask for anything for himself. At a root level, he felt that if he asked someone for something, they wouldn't love him. "That was my huge awakening," Barry explains. "God gave me the ultimate lesson in receiving. I was forced by my own health to allow the receiving process in my life."

Eventually Barry was admitted to a cancer hospital. He was terrified about the possibility of dying. At the time, he was starting the You're

My Hero™ company, which publishes an anthology series of books where people submit stories to honor everyday heroes. His intention all along had been to set up the company so that if something happened to him, the business could continue. He had the first two books in the series completed and was starting to collect the stories for the third book.

One Sunday morning, Barry woke up and found three friends standing over him. "Your goal is to heal, Barry," they told him. "We'll take care of the book for you."

"These people came out of the woodwork to help me," Barry says. "It proved to me that when you get clear on what you need, you get what you ask for but not always in the ways you expect. The lesson also taught me that God loves me, my friends love me, and all the giving I had ever done was being given back to me. Now all I needed to do was receive."

Barry's friends came through for him. When he was released from the hospital, all he needed to do was write the acknowledgments for the book. "It was the most unselfish act that I had ever received," he says.

Barry's dance with cancer changed his life. He and I discussed it again recently. "What exactly changed for you?" I asked him.

"My friends standing over me in the hospital telling me they would make sure that the third book got done—I couldn't fight receiving help like I normally would. I had to accept it. And I learned to receive in that moment. Now I can ask for money. Now I can receive the gifts of assistance. Now I can ask for what I need, and it's making a big difference in my life."

This is such an important message for abundant health. Many healers believe that all illnesses take place in our emotions before they appear in our physical being.

The law of giving and receiving is going to work on you, with or without your permission. Surrender to the reality that you can't have one without the other. You might just be saving your own life. Barry admitted that he had received exactly what he had asked for—for others to take care of him.

Be Careful What You Ask For

We do receive what we ask for, so be mindful with your asking. Make sure your thoughts, feelings, and actions are centered around what you want— not what you don't want and don't need. You are currently the result of everything you've been asking for. Watch your thoughts, because thoughts become real things. Focus on seeing, feeling, and understanding what you *need* to receive.

To What Limit Do You Allow Yourself To Receive?

To what level do you allow yourself to receive? The highest level? Or do you settle for mediocrity? No one has to settle. I attended a convention and heard Jordan Adler, a leader of a large organization of sales people talk about not settling for second best or even less. He said, "Do dogs like bones? (Most people say yes.) No, they don't. Dogs like steak! They settle for bones."

 What are you settling for in your life?

Refusing to settle for less than you want or need means **you feel worthy and deserving of having your highest thoughts and standards manifest into reality**. Do you know how Steve Jobs, founder of Apple, became one of the most successful pioneers in the world of personal computers? Because he never settled for less. He had a vision, and he stayed true to it through thick and thin.

The degree to which we can recognize,
appreciate, and accept who we are—
what's most important to us,
what our accomplishments are,
what we have done, and what we haven't done
—is the degree to which we will move forward.

When people are willing to become aware of their true essence, they accelerate their results into the realm of riches, powerful relationships, healthy lives, contributions and feel worthy and deserving of abundance.

Just How Much Are You Willing to Receive?

Five years ago, Mary Jean received a phone call from a close friend with whom she worked at a network marketing business. "Someone has just shown me something, and I want you to take a look at it," her friend told her. "It's a company I've fallen in love with—their product, their leadership. You've got to see it."

Mary Jean took a look at the business and shared her friend's enthusiasm, but she told her she didn't have the financial resources to get started. Mary Jean's friend made her an offer. "I'll pay your start-up costs," she said. "It'll be my gift to you because I believe in your potential."

Mary Jean was touched by her friend's offer because she enjoyed working with her and respected her business experience. This came at a time when Mary Jean felt she needed a new opportunity in her life, so she readily accepted the generous offer.

"Being willing to receive, accept and allow this new business arrangement was the best decision I have made toward financial independence," says Mary Jean. "As a single mom, I have created a residual income that continues to grow, and none of it would have been possible had I not been open to receiving my friend's gift and been open to a new idea."

As Mary Jean invests herself daily in this gift, she's experienced a ripple effect of giving and receiving. She's attracted a large team of people who are manifesting their dreams along with her. None of this would have been created had she not been open to receiving.

"This avenue to financial success has been the most bountiful gift," she says. "What is most inspiring about it is that every day I am doing what I love to do, and I can continue to pay the original gift forward in ongoing opportunity, support, and mentorship of the people I attract as business partners and customers. Then they pay it forward to theirs, and so on, and so on."

In allowing ourselves to receive, we become rich. What if Mary Jean had been too proud to receive the gift of financial support to get her business started, or had turned down the opportunity altogether because it meant changing the way she thought about a "job" or career? When we are open to receiving, we acquire the resources we need to elevate ourselves and others.

The Barriers to Receiving

The world-famous coach and author Robert MacPhee once told me a story to explain the barriers to receiving. He had known a woman for many years, well enough to know that she had issues with being willing to receive. She and Robert were in a workshop one day doing a milling exercise where you walk around and find a partner, and one person compliments the other. The compliment can be deep because you know the person well, or something very simple. Any compliment will do. The person who receives the compliment is required to respond in the following way: "How perceptive of you to notice." The person then has to say something else positive about himself or herself.

"The power in the activity is to practice a willingness to receive a compliment, let it sink it, then turn inward and pull something else out about yourself and share even more of your greatness," Robert told me.

This woman was Robert's partner in the activity. He noticed that she seemed very uncomfortable receiving his compliment and she couldn't respond with another compliment about herself. By not accepting a compliment, recognition, gratitude, and appreciation for all that she had done—which was a tremendous amount—it created a resistance in Robert to accept a compliment from her. "She wanted to give more, but I wasn't comfortable to receive it. It created a feeling of tension for me," Robert said. There was definitely a block in the flow of giving and receiving energy.

What I find most interesting about this story is that the woman felt resistance toward receiving a compliment and therefore received resistance from the person with whom she was partnered. We receive exactly what we give. That's the law of vibration in action. Energy vibrates with like energy. We reap what we sow. We get what we give—good or bad.

On an energetic level, people sense how we feel about ourselves and interact with us accordingly. Are you willing to receive a compliment, recognition, gratitude, or appreciation for who you are? The best way to receive a compliment is to let it in, feel it, then say "Thank you." Try taking this a step further and replying with another compliment about yourself; this is just the icing on the cake.

"Robert, you have created an incredible book and journal system with *Manifesting for Non-Gurus*," I said to him. "Thanks, Penny" was his response. "How perceptive of you to notice. I'm also a marvelous parent." Robert used his own magic on me.

Is Bragging a Turnoff?

Growing up, we were taught by parents, society, teachers, coaches, ministers, and other leadership figures not to brag about ourselves, that bragging is bad. We have strayed too far in worrying about bragging. Just because someone accepts a compliment or shares one of their strengths doesn't mean they're bragging or full of themselves.

There's another side to this: It's okay to tell the truth about ourselves. It's okay to remember what we're skilled at and what we've accomplished. We've been told not to do it—only to give and not to take—but there has to be a balance with both. Realizing what we excel at and what we love to do—and operating our lives from that point of view—powerfully projects self-love and confidence, not self-loathing and arrogance.

There is a strong, definite relationship between feeling worthy, feeling high self-esteem, and performing at our peak. When we feel good about ourselves, we produce good results. When we feel excellent about ourselves, we produce excellent results. It's okay to tell the truth about who we really are without feeling we're doing someone else wrong or bragging.

It's okay to shine—even if those around you don't shine as brightly. The world needs your brilliance, and your light will illuminate the paths of other people.

Allow yourself to receive praise, recognition, and acknowledgment. This is critical. Let others help you feel worthy and deserving by allowing their compliments to resonate deep within your soul.

More important than receiving compliments from others, is receiving them from ourselves. Praise yourself often. Several times a day. Self approval is one of the single most important confidence and self esteem fundamentals. The next chapter is dedicated to giving to numero uno— that's *you*.

> *"I can live for two months off a good compliment."*
> **—Mark Twain**

Besides opening the channels to receiving, you can ask for and invite good energy into your life.

A.S.K. and You Shall Receive

David was feeling the financial pressures of the new economy. "Will you take back my leased car and give me something else?" he asked his car dealership.

"We will," they replied and switched the vehicle, at no charge, to one he could better afford.

"Will you take less rent for our business space?" he asked his landlord.

"We can," the landlord agreed.

How many times do we struggle through challenges without asking for help? We can ask for what we need and accept the answer given.

If you ask and get "no" for an answer, you're no further ahead, but you haven't lost anything either. If you don't ask, you could lose the potential of getting a "yes."

> *"Ask, and it will be given to you; Seek and you will find; Knock, and it will be opened to you."*
> **—Matthew 7:7**

Like Barry in the story earlier in the chapter about an unwillingness to receive, sometimes people who pride themselves on being high achievers have the greatest difficulty asking others for help in times of darkness or change, but when we speak up and say, "I need your help," it magically appears, sometimes from sources we don't even realize are available to support us.

Receiving allows more love to enter our lives. When we reach out to others by asking for help, they reach back. Love and kindness can heal people's lives and bless both the giver and receiver at the same time.

Learning to ask for what you want is easier if you keep the acronym A.S.K. in mind.

<u>A</u>ssert yourself, <u>S</u>elf-worth, <u>K</u>nowledge

Many people will share with you what you want to learn from them. Assert yourself by stepping out of your comfort zone, honor your self-worth enough know you deserve to be shared with, and seek the knowledge to find out how others are achieving their dreams. Believe that you are worthy of receiving the knowledge to grow yourself. All you have to do is ASK then open yourself up to receive.

How Often Do You Turn Away
From Receiving What You Deserve?

Many gifts are given but not received. A compliment, an offer of service, an opportunity—I'm sure you can think of times in your life when someone or something was offered and at some level you wanted to say yes, but something held you back. How many times do you turn away from receiving what you've asked for or what you truly deserve only because it isn't packaged as you'd expected? The following story has been told for many years by different sources, and will help you understand what I mean.

As a young man was approaching his college graduation, he told his wealthy father of a beautiful sports car that he had admired in a dealer's showroom. He was sure his father could afford it, so he asked for the car as a graduation gift. On the morning of his graduation day, the young man was called into his father's private study. His father praised him for his good grades and told him he loved him and was very proud. The father then handed his son a gift. It was a Bible.

The son angrily raised his voice and asked, "With all your money, you give me a Bible?" He left the house and left the holy book and didn't return to his father's home for many years.

The young man became quite successful. One day, as he sat in his beautiful home, enjoying the company of his wonderful, loving family, he felt an urge to reach out to his aging father. Before he could make arrangements, however, a telegram arrived, advising him of his father's passing and stating that all of his father's possessions had been willed to him. The man left immediately to tend to the estate.

Sadness and regret filled his heart as he entered his father's study. The Bible sat on his father's desk just as he had left it many years ago. His eyes filled with tears, he opened the book and turned the pages. He found solace in the words he read.

An envelope dropped out of the book and onto the floor. It contained a car key, tagged with the name of the dealership where the sports car sat in the showroom. On the reverse side of the tag were his father's handwritten words: "Paid in full. Love, Dad."

Even though things aren't always packaged the way we expect them to be, they have been given to us for a reason.

Think of all the things you struggle with, the challenges and problems you face in your daily life. Are these gifts? Well, they certainly don't look or feel pleasant, but they are gifts. They are gifts of opportunity, gifts that change us because they force us to grow and learn and face adversity and get stronger each and every day. Don't turn away from the gifts you are presented with, even though they may not be packaged as you may have expected.

> *"All true gifts patiently wait for you*
> *until you're ready for them."*
> **—Butterfly Beth Fields**

Open Yourself Up to Receiving Feedback

The graduating man in the story was not open to receiving the feedback from his father, that the bible would be an asset to his future life. Feedback is very worthwhile. Often, it is uncomfortable to receive, especially when it pokes at our feelings, and our inner fears and insecurities. Imagine that feedback is the fuel that will propel you to grow and change. Be open to what it is—one person's opinion! It isn't necessarily right or wrong; it's just one person's opinion.

Like Carlos in this next story, who was open to receiving some life-changing feedback about his appearance, you too can benefit by the suggestions and opinions of those who care enough to encourage you.

Stephen worked as a manager in a government-funded program designed to groom unemployed people for automotive sales. It was an intensive training program that helped participants achieve personal, professional, and spiritual growth.

A man named Carlos walked in with long hair down to his shoulders and an earring in his left and right ear. Weighing in at about 280 pounds, Carlos told Stephen about his experience in carpet sales and how he had been laid off. Carlos seemed respectful and pleasant, but more important, Stephen noticed the man had a fire in his eyes, that he wanted to be something more than what and who he currently was.

"I'll make you a deal, Carlos," Stephen said. "I'll set up a second interview with you if you cut your hair, change your clothes, and take those earrings out. If you do that, then we'll consider whether you're suitable for the automotive industry or dealing with the general public."

Stephen knew his words seemed harsh and probably went against the code of conduct for managers, but he didn't want to waste time on someone he knew wouldn't stand a chance of landing a decent job without changing his appearance.

Carlos immediately stood up, shook Stephen's hand, and told him he'd be back. He immediately got himself to a clothing store, got a haircut, removed his earrings, and returned to the office two-and-a-half hours later. He waited in the reception area for Stephen to finish his scheduled interviews.

"Is there a guy out there with a really round face?" Stephen asked his secretary while she escorted the interviewees in one by one.

"Yes," she said. "He's been waiting for a while. He has a price tag on his boots."

That's Carlos, Stephen thought. It was 5 p.m. when he finished his last interview. Carlos came in with a presentable look, and he and Stephen talked for the next three hours. "I knew at that time I had a superstar in the making," Stephen says.

More than sixty people were interviewed that week, and Stephen welcomed thirty into the training program, including Carlos. "He was somewhat quiet and had a bit of a language barrier," Stephen says. "Like most new people in the sales profession, Carlos was scared—scared to make a change, afraid of rejection, and fearful that his past experiences of being fired or later let go would recur."

Due to these fears and insecurities, those new to the sales profession must let their guard down and believe in the person who's training them, Stephen explains. On the first day, Stephen had to figure out who the program participants were as people so he could learn how to approach them, engage them, and help them make it through the program.

It took Carlos a couple of days to realize that Stephen was authentic and real and that he could trust him. He completed his coursework, took the standard tests, and learned the automotive industry sales profession—from honing his personal skills and feeling self-worth, to handling meet-and-greets and closing sales.

Nineteen of Stephen's students received placements at Toyota, General Motors, Chrysler, and Kia, which gave them experience in the world of automobile sales. Carlos started to sell cars too. His start was slow at first, because he didn't like the paperwork involved, but with regular follow-up visits to bridge his learning in his new job, Stephen helped him adapt and recognize the value of all of his associated responsibilities.

Carlos sold two or three cars during his first month but later began to outperform the average salesperson; he sold ten cars, twelve cars, fifteen, then eighteen cars in a month. The general manager called Stephen to say they had a superstar in Carlos, and they couldn't thank him enough.

Carlos's career soared. He had started as an automotive sales representative, then was promoted to used car manager, then new car manager, and finally to the position of general manager for a high-end dealership. Over a period of three years, he went from collecting $365 per week in unemployment benefits to earning $250,000 a year. He even received a sports car as a bonus. For many, a career path such as this takes a lifetime.

Carlos has since chosen a new career in real estate and sells multimillion-dollar estate homes, but that's not all that has transformed. His personal self-worth grew because he realized he could find happiness in what he had to offer others in service, and his joy came from serving people rather than consuming food. He lost more than eighty pounds then met and married the love of his life.

"Carlos and I have become friends," Stephen says. "He often says, 'Steve, I will never forget you. I will always be grateful for the skills you taught me and for your belief in me, that I could create the life I wanted and deserve. Until the day I die, I will always remember your voice that guided me to where I am today.' "

If you can learn to receive feedback as a gift, you'll begin to see feedback in a whole new light — and there are many more loving gifts to unpack within it. With the lights of feedback turned on, you'll see and feel everything — the good, the bad, and the ugly. It takes courage to look deeply into the feedback we receive, and contemplation to understand why the feedback has come to us.

The circle of abundance is tuned into one channel; we cannot be selective of that which we will receive, and that which we resist. We must take it all.

This is how we fully receive. We want riches that are packaged beautifully, but we must also accept the inflow of gifts that aren't presented to us so attractively. Over time, we will see that the gifts that stretch our limits and force us to grow are the most precious gifts of all.

Make the space and time to unwrap the gifts that can be found in feedback. Reflect, think, and correct your course so that you may find your way back to your greatest path. Take regular pit stops to give and receive your own feedback, too, by listening for your soul to speak, and for feedback from your higher power.

Be Still and Be Rich

We all seek more relaxation, time outdoors, and peace in our days however, the reality is that it's difficult to mentally shut ourselves off in this digital age. We are so conditioned to life's sound bites of information that reach us through email, text messages, web media, television and radio, the workplace and our family lives, that we are forgetting how to be still, to be silent, and to find solitude. We are lacking mindfulness and attention toward our inner self.

Our lives have become so filled with noise and distraction that we have evolved to be uncomfortable with silence. For example, if someone is sitting silently in a room with you, you may ask them what's wrong or what's bothering them, since it is unusual to be with others and have long pauses or gaps in conversation. Another example is that when we aren't doing something or taking part in any mind-consuming activities, we feel 'bored' because we've lost touch with the power of silence, stillness and solitude.

"Solitude" is defined as the state of being or living alone. The word 'alone' is from Middle English literally meaning "all one" or whole. The history of the word 'alone' actually refers to a greater sense of presence with one-self, as opposed to being separate or secluded from others. A lot can be gained from living in the presence of your whole self, but doing nothing and spending time in solitude or silence has become uncommon.

How can we do nothing and become rich?

There are many benefits to silence and solitude. We can dream and create in our mind, and we can receive messages through our imagination and thoughts. In silence and solitude, we nourish our soul, recharge our energy, and receive life-giving power. Silence brings us back to wholeness and to ourselves; this is the ultimate gift to receive.

How can you be still in a life that you are so busy living?

When we feel overwhelmed with tasks and to-dos, we react by engaging in some action which is an outward use of our energy. But if we remain silent and still and make time to contemplate, we are strengthening our potential by keeping our energies within. You will have more outward power when you go inward first.

We are human beings, not "human doings." We need to give ourselves permission for non-doing and make time to just be and feel content in that space, instead of feeling guilty that we should be doing something else, or serving someone who needs us. We must feel satisfied with stillness. Sometimes being present in the moment of doing nothing *is* doing the important thing.

It's not easy. Being still and silent takes practice. Don't get impatient; set your intention on being still. Sit down, close your eyes, quiet your mind, and slow your breath; this will lull you into rest. You may be tempted to fidget—enforce the stillness, and the urge will leave. You can do this almost anywhere (unless you are driving).

The benefits are well worth the investment, and may take the form of a message you receive, or thoughts that you release; the riches you gain may be just be a mental break that you are allowing yourself, or could be a message or idea coming in for you that will result in great wealth. Sitting in what is known as 'the classroom of silence[1]' for one hour a day can help you accomplish more than you would doing tasks for several hours. It's a way to step back, look at the big picture of your life or work, and review everything without being engaged in anything. If you think you don't have time to do it for an hour a day, you most likely need it more than you think. Even 15 minutes is better than no minutes.

Some people think this is prayer.[2] Prayer is giving. Prayer is talking or sending thoughts toward your higher power. Being still and silent is the opposite—receiving. Solitude is being 'all one' with your higher self, and 'all one' with God and the energy of everything. Solitude is being open to and allowing what you need to come to you. Maybe the answers you have been looking for will finally find that landing space.

Each time you plug in your electronic devices to recharge, ask yourself "Have I given myself time to recharge?" Plug yourself into your source energy, be still, and be rich.

When we are silent, still, and present with ourselves, we can listen to our inner voice and hear our own spirit guiding us. My good friend Kody calls this guidance "promptings." The next story is told in Kody's book, *Promptings*, and is retold here with his permission.

Act on Your Promptings®

[3]The last time Kody saw his brother Kris alive was at a family gathering. Kody was leaving and ignored a prompting he'd felt to go and give his big brother a hug and tell him he loved him. Shortly afterward, Kris was killed in a work-related accident. His death was a defining moment in Kody's life

---

1   Matthew Kelly talks about 'The classroom of silence' in almost every book he has written, including *The Rhythm of Life*
2   Barbara De Angelis, Real Moments Dell 1995
3   Reprinted with permission from "Promptings: Your Inner Guide to Making a Difference," by Kody Bateman, Eagle One Publishing, LLC.

and has since enhanced the lives of millions of people, by giving them the opportunity to act on their promptings daily.

After receiving tragic news, Kody and his family headed to Kris's newly built home to visit his widowed wife and three young children. The yard hadn't been put in yet. Kody stood in the front room looking out the window.

"What I saw next was another defining moment for me," he says. "Unexpectedly, eight or nine trucks pulled into the yard, and fathers and sons started piling out of those vehicles. Picks and shovels in hand, they marched into the yard. More trucks pulled up with loads of top soil, sod, sprinkler pipe, wood for a fence, and parts for a children's swing set and playground."

Within four hours, this small army of concerned people had installed the entire yard—fence, sprinklers, grass, a swing set, and even a sandbox.

"Our family was overcome with emotion," says Kody. "No words could have ever been spoken to comfort us the way this enormous act of kindness did."

Kody walked outside and asked who had put this whole thing together. He was guided to a man who was about twenty-five years old. Kody asked him what had given him the idea to spearhead this incredible act.

The man said, "You see all these people working in this front yard? Your brother helped every one of us put in our yards."

He told Kody he was saddened by the news about Kris's death, and when driving out of their neighborhood that morning, he looked at Kris's yard and noticed that it hadn't been finished yet. He had a prompting that, come hell or high water, before the sun set over the West Mountains that night, Kris's yard would be completed.

"It was amazing to me that this young man used the same word, 'prompting,'" Kody says. "I ignored a prompting and lost a brother. I then witnessed the result of someone acting upon a prompting—a prompting that delivered an army of people to a young widow's yard and began the healing process of an entire family."

Kody will never forget the powerful impact this experience had on his life. "In that moment, I received a message loud and clear that my mission in life was to act on my promptings and help others to do the same," he explains. "I realized at that moment that there are two types of promptings. The inner prompting—the voice inside you that knows who you are—and the outer prompting—what you do with who you are."

After this incident, Kody vowed to always act on his promptings. He started a company that enables people to act on their promptings, with an online greeting card and gift service company called SendOutCards.

"We're one of the fastest growing companies in our industry," Kody says. "Promptings are being acted upon by millions of people. We are now able to give like never before."

To be able to understand our inner promptings, we must listen to our internal guidance and wisdom and be open to receiving. In order to receive internal guidance, we must make time and space to hear it. Our soul speaks quietly, and we must create a landing space for what we ask for to come in.

When we listen to our inner promptings, and act on them, we can't help but bring riches into our lives. Listening for inner promptings is a practice that, when done consistently, will instill an abundance mentality.

The Abundance Mentality

> "I believe in abundance; I desire
> abundance; I receive abundance."
> —**Shakti Gawain**

An abundance mentality basically means being of the mindset that there is plenty out there for everyone. Ask yourself the following questions to gauge whether you have an abundance mentality.

1. Do you spend a lot of time and energy competing with others or putting people down verbally because you fear that others are better than you are?
2. Are you the type of person who battles with your weight but insists on eating every last morsel of food on your plate because you don't want it going to waste?
3. Do you struggle in your business or career, thinking there isn't enough opportunity for everyone?

In these three brief examples, you see competition, judgment, and limitation. These fears come from a scarcity mentality that there is not enough.

The true nature of abundance is that it has no limits.

There are many benefits to believing there is plenty for all. When you know and feel that you deserve and are worthy of abundance—and that all people are also worthy and deserving— you can achieve win/win outcomes when making choices and decisions.

What would our lives be like if we changed our thinking to be in sync with a mentality of abundance? We would believe that the world has fruit for all; that there is plenty to go around; that there is a lot of room at the top; that we are beneath no one and also superior to no one. If we developed this mentality, we would free ourselves from fear and judgment, and accept that the world is abundant with freedom.

Let's look at the characteristics of an abundance mentality versus the opposite—scarcity. When people have a scarcity mentality, they believe there is only one pie in the world and they've got to fight to get their piece of it.

Scarcity Mentality	Abundance Mentality
Feeling you have to hoard things.	Being secure with letting go.
Believing that victory means achieving success at the expense of someone else.	Believing that victory means success with mutually beneficial results to all involved.
Difficulty celebrating people, including family, friends, and business associates.	Showering people with positive compliments, even though they are not perfect.
Difficulty sharing credit, recognition, power, and profit.	Realizing that everyone plays a part and deserves a piece of the reward.
Difficulty being a team player because differences in opinion are judged as wrong.	Accepting and appreciating the diversity of a team or group of people, and using those differences to leverage a better result.
Concern that the market for your product is saturated.	Believing that everyone is a prospect or that potential is unlimited.
Fear of shining so bright that others will be at a disadvantage.	Realizing that there is enough light and love in the world for all people to shine their brightest.

The scarcity mentality is limiting. If we have a scarcity mentality, we waste far too much energy on conflict and negative thinking and stifle our creativity. On the other hand, the abundance mentality reaches beyond one's ego. It is fearless, free, and immune to criticism. It is beneath no one and superior to no one. It is, in fact, full of magic.

What Are the Benefits of an Abundance Mentality?

Characteristics of integrity, maturity, and an abundance mentality create win/win situations for all parties involved. Win/win is a thought process of both the mind and the heart that continuously seeks mutual benefit in human interaction. With a win/win frame of mind, all parties feel good about the solutions, agreements, and decisions because they are mutually beneficial for everyone involved. In this way of thinking, you place emphasis on cooperation not competition.

How Do We Learn to Acquire an Abundance Mentality?

One of the easiest ways to shift your way of thinking to an abundance mentality is to spend time with people who already think this way. You are the product of 80 percent of the people you spend time with, so choose to spend time with people who you feel possess the qualities and characteristics you wish to adopt.

Imagine yourself as a successful, prosperous person who is very satisfied and fulfilled. You become what you think about, so choose excellent thoughts. Open your eyes to goodness, beauty, and abundance. These qualities surround you. Imagine the world transformed into a healthy and prosperous environment for everyone.

The concept of an abundance mentality eliminates our need to criticize others, pass judgment, evaluate, and analyze and label people— all of which create turbulence in our inner dialogue. An abundance mentality releases the flow of positive energy, which is essential in achieving personal success.

Let's revisit the three questions I asked earlier to determine how one's behavior might change in these circumstances with an abundance mentality.

1. Do you spend a lot of time and energy competing with others or putting people down verbally because you fear that others are better than you are? — One who believes there is plenty for all would not waste energy competing with others. He or she would look for ways to achieve win/win results.

2. Are you the type of person who battles with your weight but insists on eating every last morsel of food on your plate because you don't want it going to waste?—One who has an abundance mentality knows to eat until he or she is full, that his or her food supply is plentiful, and that discarding extra food is healthier than stuffing it in and having it stick around for the next five or ten years.

3. Do you struggle in your business or career, thinking there isn't enough opportunity for everyone?—One who believes that potential for business success is unlimited will keep mining for more opportunity, more clients, and more wealth.

Having a mentality set on abundance for all is a win/win situation for everyone. Our lives change for the better when we adopt this mentality, because we *trust* in abundance and therefore open ourselves up to its in-and-out flow.

Choose now to replace limiting thoughts that cause you to hold on to things and hoard by seeing, feeling, and experiencing abundance everywhere; it is available when you open up to receive it.

Receive Fully and Be Rich

If someone gives me a gift, and I open it, smile, and thank him or her, have I received? Not fully. If someone gives me a gift, and I open it, admire it, feel it, make space for it in my heart, understand why the giver acquired it and gave it to me, and feel and share my gratitude, then I am fully receiving.

Receiving can feel like expansion and warmth. The opposite, resistance, feels constricting and cold. In making an effort to receive all gifts fully, even though they may not be packaged the way we want them, we must open our heart, which is similar to a hand that must open so that we can put something in it. The heart only has one door, and when it is open, we feel all emotions. We can't block some and expect to fully feel others. We prosper with the least effort when we are fully open to receiving everything.

We can only continue to be great givers if we receive, thus creating the limitless circle of abundance.

CHAPTER 3

Giving to Yourself

"I seek constantly to improve my manners and graces,
for they are the sugar to which all are attracted."
—Og Mandino

Inner Abundance

Giving and growing rich is an inside job. It starts with giving to ourselves. Doing the work for this book and researching and creating programs on this topic gave me the opportunity to work hard on mending and fixing my own life. I had to learn to give more to parts of myself that were suffering. I had to look deep within myself to find my internal flaws so that I could become a better giver. Ultimately I discovered that my relationship with myself has everything to do with the quality of the relationships, opportunities, and abundance that I attract.

When I approve of myself, I approve of others. When I doubt myself, I doubt others. When I feel that others aren't contributing enough to my life, I realize that the root of the problem is that I'm not contributing enough to theirs. When I feel afraid to ask for fair pricing for my services, I realize that I'm not valuing my services enough.

The roots of our strengths and weaknesses lie in our relationship with ourselves. For example, when I did the work to nurture a better relationship with myself, my family problems began to heal. My inner self-acceptance was blocking the flow of abundance, especially love, in my immediate family.

The degree to which we love and honor ourselves is the degree to which we will receive abundance.

When I clean the lenses through which I see my world, everything becomes pure again. It really is that simple, but it's not that easy. Internal cleansing requires being aware of your imperfections and a motivation to purify them on a regular basis. The motivation part is like bathing—it doesn't last; that's why you need to do it every day!

Clean Your Windows

One July, Betty and Freddy bought a new house. Each morning they enjoyed breakfast in their new kitchen, which overlooked a beautiful backyard. One morning, Betty caught a glimpse of her new neighbour hanging her laundry out to dry.

"Oh, my word," Betty said to Freddy in disgust. "Our neighbor is hanging laundry that is stained and spotted with dirt. How terrible!"

Freddy looked down and continued to eat his breakfast.

A few days later, the couple settled down again for a leisurely breakfast. Once again, Betty looked out and saw her neighbor's laundry. "For heaven's sake, she's done it again. She hung a complete load of laundry that is absolutely filthy. Look, Freddy. Isn't that absolutely awful?"

Freddy shrugged, cocked his head with a sigh, rolled his eyes, and continued to eat.

The next morning, the couple were enjoying their usual breakfast when Betty noticed, to her utter amazement, something unusual. "Finally our neighbor has learned how to wash a load of clothes. They're clean today, Freddy. Look!"

Freddy looked up at Betty and quietly announced, "No, dear. I was up early this morning and cleaned our windows."

And so it is with our life. What we see when watching others depends on the purity of the window through which we look. You may have heard this story before, and it certainly does relate to our lives and the riches we receive. When we clean our own internal windows, we increase the clarity and purity of what we see.

There are two ways to look at this story and how it can help us attract riches. One, of course, is the idea of not passing judgment on others. The other is the importance of keeping our own windows clean. When you change the way you look at things, the things you've been looking at change.

Do the lenses through which you see the world need a cleaning? We can clean ourselves from the inside out in many ways, including spiritually, mentally, and physically. In what ways do you need a cleaning?

By using this book and taking action on the ideas, you are cleaning your windows—inside and out—so that new ideas and knowledge can guide you toward more peaceful, productive, and enjoyable relationships and permanent abundance.

"Judge not lest ye be judged."
—Matthew 7:1

Give to Yourself

We tend to spend a lot of our energy on others. Parents dote on their children and leave themselves little time for self-nurturing. Our youth are occupied with thinking about how others see and think of them. Business associates waste their energy worrying what others are doing or not doing, or saying, thinking, or earning.

 What if we invested more energy in finding out who we really are?

You can only fulfill the needs that you have deep in your soul once you remember what they are. We feel worthy of abundance when we're in alignment with who we are spiritually. When we understand that we're a part of the force that created all things, we know, without a doubt, that we are worthy. Therefore, when we nurture our own spirit by taking the time to feed it love, we find a balance of hope and honor that fuel giving and receiving our own inner abundance.

Who are you at the core of your being? If you're unclear regarding the answer to this question, try the exercise "Who Am I?" in Appendix A at the back of this book.

Find Your "Why"

When I was eighteen, I moved to the big city of Toronto, landed a full-time job, and quickly worked my way to the title of Executive Secretary to the Vice President of Sales. I saw the commission checks that the sales force were earning on a weekly basis. Holy moly! If I wanted to earn that kind of money, I had better get a loan to study and become a brain surgeon, or...get into sales. I chose the latter option, but it was just a decision at this point in my life. I hadn't taken action taken on it yet.

During lunch one day, I ventured onto Yonge Street to purchase a pair of shoes. I received excellent service at the store. I commended the sales associate for her gift of great service and then headed back to the office, happy with my purchase and my experience of being served well, and feeling pride in having verbally recognized the salesperson. I mentioned the "over and above" service I had received to Peter, my VP and boss, and Phil, another executive in his office.

"I hope you told her that her service was excellent," Phil stated.

"I most certainly did," I told him.

Within six months, Phil left the company we worked for and became the president of another. He called me personally with an invitation to join him in that business. It was a direct sales organization where I could start my own business distributing a line of kitchenware products through home party sales. "I knew you'd be dynamite at this business because you appreciate quality service and are considerate and well mannered with people," Phil told me. I accepted and embraced the opportunity.

Because of one compliment to a shoe store associate, I was sought after by Phil, now president of a new company, who displayed ample confidence in me. *Hmm. Interesting how giving compliments to others has come full circle back to me*, I thought.

My success with this company lasted for ten years, during which I moved back to my hometown, recruited, trained, and motivated a team of independent representatives. I remember my first month in the business like it was yesterday.

Day One: I headed into my home office at 9 a.m. and sat at my brand-spanking-used desk. It was completely empty, except for a phone and a pen. My chair was a crappy brown cloth thing on wheels that my dad had found at a yard sale. He thought I would need it for my office, so he dropped it off at my house when I moved in. This wasn't quite the vision of the ivory tower office I had in my mind, but you've got to start somewhere, right?

I started dialing phone numbers to let people know that I had something unique to show them and that I wanted to visit and cook dinner for them in their home. I was trying to fill my calendar with dates—not the romantic kind, just appointments where I could demonstrate my product and help people solve their cooking challenges.

I faced a high level of rejection. These were people I knew, so they did take the time to talk to me on the phone for a couple of minutes and welcome me back to town, but a lot more of them said "no" than "yes" to an in-home demonstration. Rejection was difficult for me to get used to.

One afternoon I attended an entrepreneurial workshop where we learned about having a "life purpose" or a "why" statement, which would underscore the reason we do what we do for business. I created and wrote my "why" down on paper and brought it back to my office to hang on the wall over my desk. "To help millions of people achieve their goals" was my "why" statement. It would help me put my thoughts, tasks, and challenges into perspective; stay focused; and work with purpose.

For the remainder of that first week, I focused on building the business and stayed consistent with my daily phone calls to find customers. Even though I felt awkward being rejected by people who didn't want an appointment, the "why" statement on my wall inspired me.

There was a lady named Jean at our head office. She was my lifeline. She called me regularly during my first week to see how I was doing, and that made me feel like the company cared about me. It would have been difficult to stay positive without her support. "I have three home parties booked," I said to her in excitement. "Hooray for you, kiddo," she said. "I knew you could do it."

Week Two: I drove to Manitoulin Island to do one of my first in-home demonstrations. An elderly lady and her small group of friends had gathered to learn about our elaborate line of cookware. I made a sale to my hostess, and I gave her a beautiful pink glass bowl that we called the "Rosaline bowl" as a gift for having the party. It was unique and pretty, and I was proud to offer it in appreciation before I embarked on the two-hour drive home, alone in the dark. I was excited about my new business, so driving and being alone didn't bother me. I loved my new success and progress, and I felt as if I were flying home. I felt high on life.

"I sold a full set of cookware last night," I told Jean excitedly the next morning.

"Wow. That's fantastic, Penny," she exclaimed.

Later that morning, the phone rang. It was my hostess from the previous night, calling to cancel her order and to tell me that she didn't want her Rosaline bowl either, because it was pink. She said that, having thought about it, pink doesn't match tomatoes, and she puts tomatoes in her salad and therefore finds a pink bowl useless. I didn't know what to say. It was like someone had stuck a pin in my balloon of enthusiasm, and I deflated very quickly.

All of my business enthusiasm disappeared in that moment. I agreed to tear up the contract for her cookware set and gave her my home address so she could drop off her hostess gift, because she really wanted to give it back. I picked up the receiver and called my lifeline, Jean. As I waited for her to pick up, I glanced at my "why" statement on the wall and wondered whether I would ever get over this overwhelming feeling of discouragement.

"I don't think this business is for me," I said in a disheartened tone and then told Jean what had happened.

"She was probably just having a bad day," Jean consoled me, as an excuse for why anyone could be so ungrateful about their hostess gift.

I cried. We talked. I cried some more. I was really disappointed that all the driving and time and excitement had turned into nothing.—at least nothing that I could see at the time.

For the rest of the week, the "why" statement that hung above my desk seemed to be speaking to me. I felt it pull me through my negative thoughts and into the realm of serving others. Something about that statement made me feel ambitious and capable to make a difference.

Week Three: I had my first one-hour weekly team meeting. Two people came. I gave them my best training, motivation, and recognition. I realized "To help millions of people achieve their goals" was already in progress; I had just helped two.

Giving out awards, education, and motivation at my weekly meetings became my top priority, and in doing so I discovered my greatest passion in life—motivating people to achieve their goals. A plaque hangs on my office wall today, welcoming my team into the Million Dollar Club. We earned that elite status as a group, under my leadership.

If I hadn't gone through the disappointments myself (and there were many of them), how could I teach others how to overcome the same challenges? Giving encouragement, praise, recognition, and acknowledgment was a powerful process as I developed a team of committed people who were all in business for themselves. I sure am glad I didn't quit during my second week.

By helping many others get what they wanted, I received an abundance of skills, respect and money too. I was in my very early twenties, earning 100-percent commission, to the tune of more than $50,000 a year.

The skills I learned in the direct sales/network marketing profession have been the most valuable success skills I have today. I learned not to wish things were easier, but to wish I could meet the challenges with courage and move through them. I needed to learn to be more patient with my impatient self and to be determined and persistent. Had I not had faced these challenges, I would have not learned the lessons.

> **?** How would your life change if you had a clear statement that outlined your purpose or your "why," one that you could use as a compass to guide you through emotional storms?

As I spent most of my evenings and weekends in this direct sales business, I used the daytime to work with my newfound passion of motivating people to achieve their goals. I began to teach the leadership skills necessary for success to others in seminars, keynotes, and written materials. The rest is history. You're reading this book, and I'm still helping people achieve their goals.

Make time to find your "why."

> *"When you have a WHY, you can deal with any WHAT."*
> **—Viktor Frankl**

Loving You

What if we could love ourselves enough? I mean, really love ourselves unconditionally, no matter what? No matter what is written in our past, we can get to a point of feeling that we are "enough." We are divine; we are a part of the Creator, of God, of the source energy that orchestrates all things. Therefore we are, at our core, pure light and love.

> **?** If we loved ourselves unconditionally, what kind of power would we have?
> What would the inner peace feel like?
> What could we accomplish with energy that comes from a place of love and confidence?

Imagine a life in which you unconditionally love yourself and give yourself away in service to others. Imagine a life in which you are very confident in your service and you feel deserving of fair compensation. That is the place where we give and become rich.

Richness is an inside job—one we have within our power. No one can take care of it for us. Only *we* can nurture our unlimited potential to enjoy life's abundance of riches, and it begins with the relationship within us.

The More I Shine, the Better for Mankind

Do you hold back from your greatness because you don't want other people to look worse than you? I contemplated this idea because I have become excellent at manifesting. My vision board comes to life with my desires regularly, yet I found that I wasn't feeling the joy I thought I'd feel when I reached milestones of personal achievement. On some level I was modulating how much I would allow myself to receive. After doing some work on this, I realized that I am *worthy* of receiving handsomely because I need the energy to shine, grow the tallest, produce, and share an enormous amount with others. The more I shine, the better for mankind. I cycle energy; I channel what comes to me and through me, plus what I already have within me to give out and create greatness and abundance in others. I need to shine brightly, and so do you. Since that revelation, I do not stifle my ability to receive, because I need everything I can get so that I can give back to others.

> *"We receive the light, then we impart it.*
> *Thus we repair the world."*
> —**Kabbalah**

The Importance of Self-Praise

No matter our position in life, most of us feel that it isn't proper to acknowledge our own talents and attributes. If you can't take pride in yourself, however, how can you expect others to? If you cannot compliment yourself or recognize your strengths and celebrate them, why should anyone else? You don't have to shout praise, recognition, and acknowledgment of yourself from the rooftops, but you can give it to yourself in silence or prayer, in gratitude, when journaling, and when you are speaking of yourself.

> *"Don't put a question mark where God put a period."*
> **—Joel Osteen**

Receiving Praise

When you regularly catch people doing things right and congratulate them or communicate your appreciation, you create a wave of wonderful feelings—and those feelings will be returned to you.

 When praise comes back, do you accept it?

Some people have difficulty receiving and accepting praise. They try to discount themselves because they don't feel worthy of feeling super-excellent. My best advice is to respond to praise with two simple words: "Thank you." Accept compliments and praise. After all, it's one person's opinion—and one that you cannot dispute.

When Lynn says, "The office smells fresh and clean today, Joe," he could discount himself by wondering, *Does she think it's not clean every day?* The best response is, "Thank you, Lynn."

Practice giving and receiving compliments daily. Too often we overlook what is and look for what is not. By praising, recognizing, and acknowledging ourselves daily, we vibrate out our own credibility. By receiving compliments daily, we fuel our own self-worth.

Be Grateful

One of the easiest ways to start feeling good is to count your blessings.

> **?** What are you thankful for? Can you make a list? How many items can you list? One hundred? Several hundred? Perhaps thousands?

Read your list daily and begin each item on your list with "I am thankful for…" Here are some examples:

- I am thankful for my connection to Source energy.
- I am thankful for my vigorous health.
- I am thankful for my family.
- I am thankful for the opportunities I have to use my talents to serve humanity.
- I am thankful for this time to pause and reflect.

Through frequent repetition and reminders of all that you are thankful for, you will attain a better high-vibration energy. You will attract other high-vibration energies as well. For example, income opportunities, better health, and admirable people will be attracted to you, as if you were a magnetic force.

Gratitude is the memory of your heart. Listen for it, honor it, believe in it, and let it shine in your life.

You Are the Wind Beneath Your Wings

What do you think and say to yourself and about yourself? Take note, because positive self-talk is critical to giving yourself a foundation for receiving abundance. When you know what you want, you create the vision of your life in your mind. When a challenge appears, do you tell yourself or others, "I'm so stupid," "This is too hard," "I can't afford that," "No one has that kind of money," "I never win anything," or "My thighs are too fat"? These thoughts do not serve you. Be vigilantly aware of your self-talk—it must be in line with what you want.

You can change your language to reflect what you want in your life. For example, you can tell yourself, "I am smart enough," "This is possible with effort," "I am choosing not to spend my money on this," "I am attracting money," "I am very lucky," "I am fit, fun, and fabulous," and so forth. These thoughts will attract abundance as you stop limiting yourself in disbelief with your words, both internally and externally.

Right inside of you, you have everything that you need to be, do, and have anything that you put your intention and attention on. You are whole. There is nothing missing within you. Try to remember your wholeness. You will receive riches that directly match the quality of the thoughts and feelings you have about yourself and the spoken words you use to describe yourself. Choose them all wisely. They will be the wind beneath your wings to help you soar to new heights or take you to new lows. The choice is yours.

Look at the difference in the following self-talk and recognize what empowering words sound and feel like.

DISEMPOWERING Words	EMPOWERING Words
I'm so stupid.	I'm smart enough to know what I know.
This is too hard.	I can figure this out.
I can't afford that.	At this moment, I choose not to use my money that way.
No one has that kind of money.	I will attract this money if I really need it.

I never win anything.	I am getting luckier every day.
My thighs are too fat.	I am getting more fit and healthy every day.

Why do we choose to use disempowering words to sabotage ourselves? Is it because we are wounded from past experiences, and we gather evidence to support the walls we have built around our hearts to protect us?

Give Yourself Healing Time

There are times when a professional can give you the guidance you need to help you heal, or help you choose better thoughts. Vanessa works as a massage therapist. A young woman named Sally came to her seeking healing for the pain she felt in her back.

"Through the Somato Emotional Release process," Vanessa says, "it was discovered that the discomfort was stored energy regarding her relationship with her mother, which had been broken for many years."

Vanessa used a process of dialogue in which she acted out the role of Sally's mother, and Sally expressed her feelings to Vanessa. As a result, Sally let go of the energy that had caused her pain. It left her body immediately, and she expressed that she felt happy.

About two weeks later, as Vanessa walked out of the treatment room, an older woman approached her. "Are you Vanessa?" she asked.

"Yes, I am," Vanessa told her.

"I just came to thank you and bless you for helping my daughter, Sally," the woman said, and hugged Vanessa. "Since you helped her, she has reached out to me. We've rekindled our connection. You helped me get my daughter back, and there's no better gift in life than rebuilding a broken family relationship. Bless you!"

"I was overwhelmed with emotion and felt affirmed that I am serving my purpose by helping others heal," Vanessa says.

"When we act from the heart, the results are tenfold."
—**Vanessa Brown**

Healing Yourself Has a Ripple Effect

Do you have relationships that need healing? Perhaps a family breakup or a difficult situation from the past is holding you back. Often the negative energies we hold on to manifest into physical ailments.

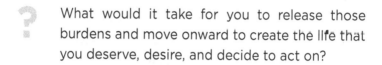

> What would it take for you to release those burdens and move onward to create the life that you deserve, desire, and decide to act on?

Burdens that you carry have a story to them. What if you could shine the light on the story from a different perspective? If you can redo the story on paper or in your mind, and see it from a different angle with a good result for yourself, you can set your burdens free. It is human nature to gather evidence to support the stories in our mind. For example, if I was taught as a child that money doesn't grow on trees and that life is a struggle and that you have to work very hard for your money, then the daily evidence I would gather would support my beliefs. Perhaps I would find a penny on the street and feel like it was too much work to bend down and pick up such a pittance. Maybe I would settle for a job that didn't fulfill me but paid me enough to struggle along, and I wouldn't look at other income opportunities because I wouldn't want to work hard.

If I decided to make a mental shift regarding money, I could find a new perspective about the way I was raised and rewrite the story. I could tell myself, *Because I grew up feeling lack and limitation regarding money, I'm now committed to doing things differently so I can attract wealth and enjoy a rich life.* I haven't changed the facts; I've just changed my perspective. In doing so, I'll be able to gather new evidence toward money. If I find a penny on the street, I can think, *I'm so abundant that money is falling from the sky and onto my path.* When an earning opportunity knocks, I can see myself as being successful and helping other people, so I would take action.

Gathering evidence will continue to reinforce your new thinking, and you can make an amazing transformation in yourself, provided the story you tell yourself is positive and expands you, and not negative, which will limit or constrict you.

I rewrote stories to replace several past experiences for myself, and I haven't looked back. When I'm tempted to tell myself the old story, I catch myself and remember the work I did to redo the story in my mind; I gather evidence to support the new story because I remember my "why"— my desire for wanting and deserving the new perspective.

It's worth doing what is necessary to heal yourself, or to look to a therapist for assistance. Releasing old tensions creates a ripple effect that will be felt throughout many generations, just as Sally and her mother experienced.

Your thoughts and feelings are at the root of your relationship with yourself, which provides the foundation of the relationships you have with others. Give yourself the time and energy you need to heal your mind, body, and spirit, just like Hariett did in this next story.

Hariett and Sarah were partners in a ladies' clothing store many years ago. Upon arriving to work one morning, Hariett's partner greeted her with the news that she wanted out of the partnership and offered to buy Hariett out of the deal.

As you can imagine, it's difficult to receive such news with an objective mind, so Hariett's emotions got the best of her. Although she agreed to sell, she was devastated.

Three weeks later, Hariett entered a different clothing store, and a sales associate immediately noticed there was something wrong—something was hurting Hariett. The associate offered her assistance.

"I sense that you're in pain," she said softly to Hariett.

"Yes, I am," she admitted. "I've had a pain much like a thorn in my finger on my right hand, and it's been bothering me for weeks."

"We digest all experiences, and holding on to the negative ones can make us sick," the woman replied, taking Hariett by the hand and gently holding her sore finger. "The pain you're holding will be released when you can let go of whatever is bothering you. There's something here surrounding forgiveness that you must take care of."

On her way home, Hariett stopped by her old store to apologize to her ex-business partner. "I put you through a lot of pain," she said, "and I want you to know I'm sorry for any hurt I've caused you."

The partnership never did rekindle, but the pain subsided immediately, and Hariett and Sarah are still friends twenty-five years later.

It's important to allow ourselves to be visible and vulnerable to others. When we let ego and fear of failure to get in the way of who we really are, it can cause us—and others—great pain.

Soul information is stored in our bones, and the hand bones are the river of expression bones.[4] Once Hariett was able to express herself, the pain stored in her finger subsided. Healing ourselves means being honest with ourselves and seeing the gift in every experience. As it turned out, leaving the business and moving on to another career was an invaluable gift for Hariett—one that would not have come to be without her former partner's request.

We need to take responsibility for making relationships work and for making an effort to resolve conflict. When we give resolution to others, we actually resolve an internal battle between our ego and our self.

What is the currency of vibrant health and pain-free living worth to you?

---

4   Andrew Raymer, author of *Revelations for a New Millennium*, 1997

What Do You Expect?

My dad always told my mom and his closest friends that I could fall into a bucket of dirt (he used a different word) and come out smelling like a rose. That's an old expression that depicts how some people can make the best of any situation, and you can too.

It all starts in your mind. What do you expect to happen in your life? Do you expect that life isn't fair? Or that people will try to rip you off? Or that life is a struggle? Or that money doesn't grow on trees? Or that rich people are evil? Or that you aren't very smart? Do you think you're just an average person, secretary, civil servant, waitress, stay-at-home mom, teenager, or senior citizen? (Note: J.K. Rowling, author of the bestselling *Harry Potter* books, was a single mother on welfare before she wrote her first book.)

These negative expectations of ourselves are called "limiting beliefs." If you believe you aren't worthy, smart enough, or deserving of life's riches, you limit yourself with your belief system. Sure, you may have been taught these beliefs from someone else or some experience in your life, but who's in charge? You are! You're responsible or *response-able*—able to choose your response to anything—from this point forward in your life.

Setting your expectations means determining what you want in your life.

 What do you expect from life?

I expect that "everything works out more perfectly than I could have imagined," and it always does. Sometimes I have to change my perspective to see the perfection in each circumstance, but knowing I'm able to choose my response gives me power and control over my thoughts and feelings.

Roses and Thorns

One weekend, my fiancé and I set out on a canoeing trip. Our route followed part of a historic waterway called the Nipissing Voyageur Passageway, on which natives brought European explorers into the interior of the continent in 1610. During our three-day adventure, we intended to enjoy nature and explore the breathtaking scenery of the route traveled by the voyagers. Our canoeing trip involved a series of lakes, rivers, and portages.

After a full day of paddling, we arrived at a lake with a very rocky shoreline. Exhaustion and muscle fatigue told us we needed to find our overnight camping spot, but there was none in sight, just rocks and trees. Finally, like a mirage, a grassy point came into sight, so we landed and set up our campsite for the night. Within half an hour, a man arrived on a watercraft and said, "You can't camp here. This is my grandfather's property, and he doesn't allow others to use it." Perhaps it had been a mirage after all, we thought.

Disappointed, hungry, and tired, I took a chance, believing that everything would work out more perfectly than I could imagine. At this point we didn't even have a fire going yet, so I was willing to try anything.

I asked the man, "Do you think there's a chance your grandfather would reconsider?"

"You can ask him yourself if you want," he answered, then led me through the bush trail to meet his grandfather.

A family reunion was taking place, and I was led to an elderly man who sat in a rocking chair. I smiled and asked very politely if he would allow us to camp on his grassy point for the evening. I explained that we had just completed a long day of paddling and couldn't find another place to rest for the night.

"You must respect the land and leave it just as you found it," the man said and granted me permission. I reached out to shake his hand or give him a hug—whatever he would accept— and he insisted that I take back two plates of hot food from the buffet table. My fiancé was delighted to see me return safely with permission to camp— and dinner!

There's a reason why I can fall into a bucket of dirt and come out smelling like a rose— that's what I expect of my life, and I give roses to others every chance I get. My expectations are only of myself, and I formulate them intentionally, with clarity and optimism. My positive and highest thoughts don't always come naturally, so I have to work at them daily.

My thoughts are like a mental rose garden. I tend to my roses every day, pruning for improvement and accepting the thorns. I expect myself to grow in a positive way with every experience and encounter.

 Which of your thoughts need pruning?

Everything Works Out More Perfectly Than I Imagine

The universe carefully orchestrates everything in my life to work out more perfectly than I could have ever imagined. Why me? Because that's what I believe and that's what I think about. Even in challenging situations, I recognize the silver lining of the cloud, the "bless in the mess," and find solace in my mind that everything is exactly how it is supposed to be.

I try to think about and imagine fantastic things. I have a personal journal; it's about fifty handwritten pages of goals; things that I want to be, do, and have; positive notes; quotes; and affirmations. This is how I design my life. In other words, I do my homework. I make time to clarify and study what I want, read my journal, remember what's important, keep myself on track, meditate, work on my self mastery program and just *be.*

? Are you clear on what you want?

There are three reasons why people are not living the life that they desire. One is that they aren't clear about what they want; the second is that they haven't decided to take action to obtain it, or the third, they somehow have conflict surrounding the process or the results.

One day I met with my business coach, Andrew. I was trying to hold back my tears, but the tap was on, and they were flowing down my face before I'd even sat down.

"Penny, why are you so upset?" he asked. He had never seen this side of me.

I placed two piles of files in front of me on the table. One pile contained financial information for a profitable business I had owned and operated for more than twenty-five years. The other pile contained the business plan and client files that proved my success in a second business I had established and worked at for the last ten years.

"I can't do both anymore," I explained to Andrew. "I feel like I've hit a plateau and taken both companies as far as I can take them together. Now I must decide. To expand either business and be really strong and profitable, I have to let one go."

"Which one makes money?" he asked.

I pointed to one of the piles. "This one."

"Which one do you love?"

My eyes welled up again as I pointed to the other pile.

"Then close the business that's making you money, and follow your heart and your passion," he advised.

"But what about money?" I asked.

"What's the worst thing that can happen?"

"No money, no income. What about my expenses?" The sound of it stressed me even further.

"So what? Who cares? What's the worst that can happen? Will your kids go hungry?"

"No, I don't think it would get that bad."

"So give it up. Chase your dreams. Take a chance, invest in yourself, and go for it."

I took Andrew's advice. I decided to chase my dreams, and this book is a big part of that picture. I was clear on what I wanted, and I knew that running two businesses wouldn't allow me the time to take action on my decision.

So I gave up one of the businesses—the one that made more money. I gave it up to become rich in other ways. The conflict that surrounded my decision was a conflict about money. I thought I needed money to be who I wanted to be. But I didn't need money. I just needed to change my conflicting thoughts about money. Today you are holding this book, and that's proof that everything works out more perfectly than I imagine. I am doing the work I love—and making plenty of money. Sometimes giving means learning to say no, or learning to let go of something that no longer serves you.

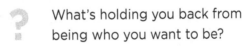

What's holding you back from
being who you want to be?

Between any situation or circumstance and your response lies your freedom to choose. You can choose how to live your life, despite your past and present situations. This power to choose is demonstrated in the next story.

Forgive and Be Rich

Merle Assance-Beedie lived her idyllic childhood years in Christian Island, Ontario, with loving parents, but she was abruptly confronted with internment in a series of four residential schools, starting at the age of five. These residential schools were operated for aboriginal children during the 20th century for the purpose of educating them in the English language, converting them to Christianity, and discouraging their native ways of life. In these schools, many First Nations, Metis, and Inuit children were deprived of loving homes and endured sexual, physical, and mental abuse, along with cultural assimilation.

Merle survived the four different residential schools and was released at the age of sixteen. She went on to heal and live in a traditional native culture despite her horrible experiences. Eventually she had a family of her own and was able to give others knowledge and examples of how to live in kind and respectful ways.

Merle, a very humble Ojibway woman (Anishinabe Kwe), became active in making positive contributions by giving people information about residential school life. Her approach was gentle, and despite her own traumatic experiences, she was able to communicate and share her ideas and opinions without a negative emotional charge.

She made a conscious decision to choose to think about kindness and respect for good relationships. Her ideology and belief for good relationships involved treating people with a kind heart, which was translated from the word "Canada" or "Kina Da," which means "Everything has heart; everything has truth."

Throughout Merle's lifetime of contributions as a nurse and as a volunteer on boards that serve her people, her door was always open to empower those in need. Her reflection always rooted back to her traditional and spiritual way of thinking, speaking, and feeling with a kind heart. She empowered people to carry on her legacy of being gentle, kind, and loving, and living as though family meant everything—because it does. Blood relatives and strangers alike adopted her as an aunt. Merle's ability to connect with people was her gift to the Anishinabek nation. Over time, she became known as Aunty Merle to many.

Merle often brought tears to the people who heard her speak, although she never had to elaborate on the cruelties she had endured in residential schools. Her voice carried the impact. She had an unshakeable conviction that kindness and compassion are much better solutions than hate and revenge.

Merle educated the general public, government, and other residential school survivors with a speech titled "The Missing Chapter: What You Didn't Learn About Aboriginal Peoples in School." The following is a powerful excerpt from Merle's presentation to the Royal Commission on Aboriginal People in 1993. It teaches us how to apologize and how to move forward.

As Anishabe people we try for balance and harmony from birth until we go through the Western door. This balance and harmony is our role in life, so we live every day toward this positive way.

When relationships turn sour, what is the healthy thing to do? We apologize. We say, "I'm sorry. Let's start over." That is basic, but fundamental to the process of change inside the relationship, whether it be a marital relationship, with children, teacher, or student. When you say, "I'm sorry," you begin on another positive note.

Victims of abuse must talk to their perpetrator to say, "This is what you did to me." The perpetrator then has the opportunity to respond, and the healthy response is, "I'm sorry. How can I make amends?"

As survivors of the residential schools and their families of children and grandchildren, we need to hear this from the intellectuals of this country, the educators, the religious organizations, health professionals, doctors, nurses, social workers, police, and others. Until we get this response, we cannot move forward toward healing.

We, too, must say, "I'm sorry too, and I forgive you."

Merle paid a visit to a dying clergyman who had abused her during her childhood. "This is what you did to me," she explained in full detail.

He apologized to her. Her last words to him were, "I'm sorry too, and I forgive you."

As a result of making that conscious decision early in her life to choose to think only about kindness and respect for genuine relationships, Merle was able to forgive and received the riches of a full life. Through her having practiced love, kindness, and respect, Merle's legacy lives on to create a positive ripple effect on the relations between the Anishabe and all races.

"Be as good as you are."
—Merle Assance-Beedie

Adversity Turned Inside Out

In every adversity that appears in your life, you can find an opportunity if you look for it. Find the cloud's silver lining. If you focus on the lesson or the opportunity of the challenge you face, you'll have the fuel to get over it and even grow from it. Merle Assance-Beedie's daughter, Lisa, said that she and her siblings often wondered what their mother's rich life would have been like had she not endured adversity.

 What adversities ultimately have provided richness and opportunity in your own life?

"The truest greatness lies in being kind,
The truest wisdom in a happy mind."
—Ella Wheeler Wilcox

Give to Your Mind

You are exactly where you are today because of the reality you have created in your mind. Think back five years ago and ask yourself what you wanted at that time, and then realize how you got it. Your thoughts made it happen. This is the potential of your mind, but are you using thoughts and feelings to create what you want? Or are you using your mind and thoughts to create what you *don't* want?

What you think about you bring about. Choose your thoughts very wisely, because you can never rise higher than them. What you do with your mind is your choice. You can choose to use your mind in a conscious, positive way, toward your goals and in line with your heart, or you can choose exactly the opposite. You must first admit that you have a choice. Then you need to be clear on what you want. Once you know where you want to go with your life, you can determine how to get there.

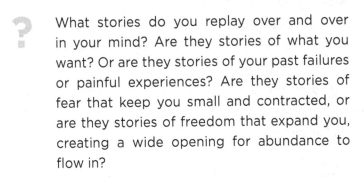

> What stories do you replay over and over in your mind? Are they stories of what you want? Or are they stories of your past failures or painful experiences? Are they stories of fear that keep you small and contracted, or are they stories of freedom that expand you, creating a wide opening for abundance to flow in?

Your stories are like videos you play time and again in your mind. Do these stories serve you? Do they help you move toward who you want to become, or do they hold you back? If your stories are holding you back, you must create a new mental video, a new story with a new perspective that offers you enormous abundance.

Set Yourself Free

Freedom is a deep and wonderful subject. Financial freedom is something many people strive for. Money is one form of energy, yet freedom regarding *all* other energy is critical in tapping the circle of abundance.

Freedom from fear, for example, can speed up the flow of all riches. Freedom from doubt can ensure a clear flow of incoming and outgoing abundance. Freedom from anger, isolation, impatience, self-punishment, guilt, shame, irritation, feeling overwhelmed—imagine living a life this free!

Changing the story of your life—past and present—is an effective way to experience more freedom. This requires letting go of old patterns that drive you to think and behave the way you do. Imagine how greatly you can receive without the blockage of fear, doubt, anger, isolation, impatience, etc. Think of the process of letting go as being like a hoarder who wants new or different furniture. The delivery truck comes to the house, but the furniture can't come through the door because there isn't space for it and the doorways are all blocked with baggage.

> Have you ever thought of how your life would be different if you weren't living with the attachment to your story of old wounds?

The thought of this is frightening, because we've spent years building walls of protection to guard us from our stories, and in the process we've created our patterns and habits. Take them away, and you feel raw and vulnerable because you see your naked truth. Resting in the discomfort of your natural, crude, unrefined self is a powerful place to be. You can see where you've been and figure out how to live without your stories that bound you in the past. Along the way you'll see many open doors. Some doors will even close.

When you begin to break free from your old story and be more authentic with who you really are, some people in your life will try to hold you back. Change is not only uncomfortable for you, but it's also awkward for those in your life who aren't steering the change. Expect this, honor others for where they are in their journey, and stay true to yourself.

Be patient with change as you transform. The freedom you will feel by being true to yourself will be gratifying. Remember that those in your life who mind don't matter, and those who really matter won't mind.

Stuck in an Unhappy Place?

I meet many people who feel stuck in an unhappy place. Their job, their relationship, or their health are not serving them well, but they're reluctant to make a shift. They're unfulfilled in one or more key areas of their life, yet they know there's something better for them. People think that the "something better" is "out there," but the truth is that it's "in here." We already have everything we need to flow through life freely; it just needs to be found, reclaimed, practiced, and polished.

A career takes an unexpected break or a relationship falls apart—these are real issues of our times. If you were walking inside a corridor and a door closed, preventing you from moving in the direction you were walking, would you find another door? Of course you would. But in these similar scenarios of life, making giant leaps out from a comfortable routine seems daunting, even though staying in the bad situation brings suffering.

How do we lift the heavy chains that bind us to these issues? Some just give up on their existing situation and move on to the next person, the next job or the next flavor of discomfort. This would be like jumping out of the window in the corridor, rather than looking for other doors through which to enter or exit. The problem with jumping to leave behind unsatisfying situations is that the problem often follows you. You think the other person was to blame, or the boss, the company, your manager, or your mother-in-law but it's likely that the issues are with 'in' you. You see them reappear no matter what the new circumstance and it's frustrating because you really haven't run from anything. You can't run from yourself.

Often, the key to leaving your unhappy place forever, is to look at how well you are receiving. Are you blocking the other person's love? Are you resisting someone at the office because you need to feel in control? Are you setting circumstances up for failure because at some unconscious level you don't feel worthy and deserving of an abundant life? These are deep questions to ponder.

When we are resistant to receiving the flow of all energy, there is a blockage in the circle of abundance.

? What is your freedom worth to you?

Would you give up your old story about why you can't be successful, change your routine, invest in yourself with time each day or night consistently for the next few years, and build a new empire to support you for a lifetime? Financial freedom and *all* freedom is within your reach. You deserve it, and you can do it, but you must decide and then take deliberate, consistent action to put your stake in the ground and leverage your efforts for a new future.

Are you willing to make an investment in yourself? Time, books, seminars, coaching, mentoring, and long-term programs are all available to you. I offer great products for all of these self-development options because I've learned that all overnight successes have been twenty years in the making, and those who have invested in their personal development soar in comparison to those who do not. If you bought a fixer-upper house, you'd invest money into it so you could live more comfortably in it, right? Maybe you'd even increase the property value, turn the property over, and make some money on the sale. Investing in yourself is no different. Why do so many people hesitate to invest in their own mastery? Your investment is bound to come back to you in leaps and bounds. The universe has a perfect accounting system. Trust it. Don't be stingy with the amount you invest in your own personal development, because it will return to you a hundred times over, in ways more perfectly than you ever could have imagined.

When One Door Closes

? How many opportunities pass you by because you're afraid to open a new door and step onto a new path?

When one door closes, another one is available and waiting for you to open. *Trust* is one of the greatest gifts you can give to yourself. Trust is your ticket to freedom, and the reason why you can't afford to live a life disconnected with your own spirit is that you need your own trust. Your spirit will guide you, even in the most difficult times, when a cloudy mind cannot see through the fog of a dilemma. Your inner flame always will ensure that there are lights on so that your path will be illuminated. When you can shine your light on a cloud from a different angle, you may create a silver lining.

The Silver Lining

The silver lining of a cloud is a metaphor for finding positivity despite an adversity or a negative situation. "If you can't find a positive in any situation, you're not thinking hard enough. It's mind over matter," I said in a seminar.

A young lady in the large audience stood and asked, "What positive can you find in losing a child?"

The room went silent.

I was struck with compassion. Even as a professional speaker with years of experience and training, I couldn't find the words to answer her question. So I turned the question to the audience. "Can anyone here help? What positive can be found in losing a child?"

After several moments of silence, the woman who had asked the question stood again. "I may have discovered my own answer" she said. "The positive result from losing my child is that I've dedicated the rest of my life to finding a cure for the disease that took her when she was only five years old."

What a brilliant answer—and one that demonstrated how the silver lining of giving in service to find a cure set her free from the pain of feeling helpless.

Your Life's Purpose

"So what's my purpose?"

Patrick Fortin stood at the large picture window that overlooked the back yard when he asked his mother this question. It was the only time in twenty-two years that she had seen his lips quiver from fear and doubt.

Patrick was one of the first Canadians to be infected with HIV. While undergoing a treatment for hemophilia (a condition that makes blood clotting difficult), when he was only seven years old, he had been exposed to tainted blood that carried the virus. At that time, in the late 1980s, not much was known about HIV, except that in advanced stages it turned into AIDS. He had been diagnosed with a death sentence at age seven.

His parents, Christine and Christian, made the decision not to be bitter. For the sake of their family and their own relationship, they chose to accept what had happened and to be grateful for what they had. In short, they decided to live life optimistically.

Living with HIV, and later AIDS, was a daily struggle for Patrick, but he accepted it and made sure to find happiness wherever he could, living each day to its fullest. He never once asked, "Why did this happen to me?" He only felt that his story could help others. To this end, Patrick visited local high schools in his community to talk about HIV, AIDS, and hemophilia. He made his message clear: HIV is 100-percent preventable and one day the world will be free of HIV and AIDS.

Patrick initiated a dialogue about subjects that weren't discussed at the time and helped to break barriers. Putting effort toward his purpose of helping others avoid the same illness brought light to his days.

At age twenty-three, after a long battle with AIDS complications, Patrick's journey ended, yet his legacy lives on. The organization Patrick4Life AIDS Awareness and Education grew from his community's desire to honor his life and to specifically communicate the desires of Patrick's dream to stop the spread of HIV and find a cure for AIDS. Through educational activities, community events, and special presentations, more than ten thousand children have been educated in the ten-week Partici-Patrick program since its inception in 2006.

In an interview with Patrick's mother, Christine, I asked how she had grown during the seventeen years she had spent caring for Patrick during his illness, and how grief affected her outlook on life.

"What does the concept of 'give and be rich' mean to you?" I asked her.

"We don't grow rich knowingly," Christine said. "We grow rich in becoming who we are, and it's not always what we imagine. Without searching for riches, and by accepting the challenges that we had to face, we have acquired skills that have brought us love and abundance. We decided that despite Patrick's diagnosis we were going to live in a positive way and be grateful for what we did have."

"What gifts do you feel you were given?"

"We were overwhelmed daily with support by our family, friends, and community. It seemed that the energy we needed was coming from outside sources. Food, pictures drawn by my music students, even people who would come to the door to support and encourage us— they were all gifts that constantly flowed into our lives and gave us tremendous energy."

Christine continued, "After Patrick's life, my husband and I started running marathons. We were not athletes, but we somehow had the energy to qualify for the Boston Marathon three times. We found ourselves being in top shape, with balance, health, and harmony in our lives."

"Where do you feel this energy has come from?" I asked her.

"I feel I have a responsibility to carry on Patrick's legacy and desire for zero AIDS and that I can live up to it. In this undertaking, I have escaped 'victim mode' and have received a grand amount of energy. In all the giving of myself, I am receiving an incredible abundance."

"How did you use strategies of gratitude to overcome this adversity and create a powerful organization that makes such a difference?"

"Accepting Patrick's illness was the first step," Christine said. "Deciding not to be bitter was the second. There was an automatic strength in the fact that I had gratitude for everything else—for my husband to be able to go to work every day, for the health of our other children, and much more. I saw God and beauty everywhere."

"Where did your strong faith come from?"

"I was raised Catholic with a fairly strict upbringing of making time for church on Sundays, and two parents who were very much in love with each other. Living in the influence of love was a pillar of strength in my early years, which I carried into my own family."

"What have you received on this journey?"

"Besides lots of positive energy from the love and support and indescribable outside sources, I have learned how to receive, learned how to say no, and learned how to let go."

"Can you give me an example of letting go?"

"Letting go of our bitterness—and our ego—was key. We underwent some counseling to help us deal with Patrick's illness. My doctor said, 'Christine, you don't have to expect yourself to be functional through all of this,' and I disagreed. I think it is important to remain functional through the challenges that we face. Letting go of the need to be perfect has given us strength to maintain a functional family through this adversity."

Christine continued, "The doctor said to me, 'I notice you've been crying the past couple of visits. Perhaps it's time for you to take some medication for depression.' And I replied, 'So we have to go through all this without being sad? I just can't visit you once a month to tell you how brutal this has been? I have to take a pill now? Do you expect me to go through this and not feel sorrow?' Although I never did agree to medication, I really felt like I needed to honor my feelings and accept them."

The growth that Christine underwent enabled her to spearhead Patrick4Life and, in doing so, raise awareness about HIV/AIDS, advocate for change in Ontario's education system, and touch the lives of more than 10,000 elementary students so far.

Though her work could never replace the loss of Patrick, the idea that a silver lining could exist in a situation so dire and painful turned out to be true and provided Christine, her family, and her community with a tremendous amount of healing.

"Nothing is impossible to a willing heart."
—Thomas Heywood

Exterior abundance begins with interior abundance. Our personal economy or worth is directly proportionate to our perception of our own value. This chapter's purpose was to shine the light on how permanent abundance can only move in when we clean our windows and see the truth about ourselves, how amazing and deserving we are of the greatest lives, and why we need to be rich in all the ways that really matter. Dirt happens. We can't expect that life will be a bouquet of roses all the time, so we must learn to navigate around the thorns. Healing— including forgiveness of ourselves and others—is part of everyone's journey here on earth. We can choose abundance when we commit to our freedom and realize that in every circumstance lies our ability to choose our response. Having a strong purpose or "why" gives us direction and meaning and will help us stay on course, even—and sometimes especially—when the going gets tough. With gratitude and self-love, anything is possible, so investing in the rich information in this chapter will give you powerful leverage to tap into the circle of abundance you so deserve. Confidence comes from finding your gift and living it. Those gifts are not material things, although they return abundant energy with which you can really enjoy material things.

"Judge your security not by what you have
but what you can live without."
—unknown

The real security you have is within yourself, and when you shine brightly, you can receive big. When you receive big, you end up with plenty of resources to create a rich life with deep and satisfying relationships, both personally and in business, to share with others. The next chapter will help you be a great giver to others.

CHAPTER 4

Giving to Others

> *"The best way to find yourself is to
> lose yourself in service to others."*
> **—Gandhi**

There are countless ways to give to others. Let's start by recognizing what people want most: love and belongingness, self-worth, support to be who they are, and recognition in honor of who they've become. You can give these blessings to people through time, words, attention, belief, trust, money, prayer, or other gifts.

These next pages will give you some ideas to build and nurture stronger relationships at home, in your community, and in your workplace. You'll see how the power of compassion and connection builds character and leadership in yourself and others.

Basic Human Needs

The value of helping others feel self-worth cannot be underrated or overstated. People who feel good about themselves produce good results. Likewise, people who produce good results feel good about themselves. It's a circle of abundant motivation that provides fuel to propel anyone toward his or her full potential.

Psychologist Abraham Maslow's hierarchy of needs helps us to better understand the process of human motivation and personal development. First on Maslow's hierarchy is food and shelter, followed by safety, and then **love and belongingness,** which includes family, affection, relationships, and work groups.

Without a satisfactory feeling of having the need of love and belongingness met, we have less or no motivation to strive to reach our higher levels of needs, which are self-esteem and self-actualization. For example, a manager would have difficulty motivating an employee to reach peak productivity if the employee did not feel a sense of belonging on the team. A parent would have trouble motivating a child to behave properly if the child did not feel unconditionally loved.

On your journey to realize your full potential, you must feel satisfied in your relationships at home and at work. We are creatures of emotion with a deep need for love. In your professional and personal lives alike, the best way to get love is to give it away. In this chapter we will learn how to love at home, how to celebrate the best in people, and how to practice love in the workplace.

People Need Love

"It is possible to give without loving,
but it is impossible to love without giving."
—Richard Braunstein

Love increases our performance and is universally recognized and celebrated around the world. There are takers of love, and there are givers. Takers, for instance, ask why you haven't called in a long time. They've been waiting for your call. Givers, on the other hand, pick up the phone and call those they are thinking about. Life gives to those who give and takes from those who take. Therefore, if you want love, you must love. When you feel a lack of love, you must give more love out.

As counterproductive as it might seem to give when we feel we are lacking, we must understand that we feel an absence of something when our spiritual self is not nurtured. When you give of yourself to others (e.g., give back time to your community, volunteer your time toward an initiative you feel strongly about, or spend time in a soup kitchen or food bank), you'll receive that which you seek, because having given, you'll feel as though you have received in the process. You are always giving and receiving simultaneously.

Love is the glue that bonds people together, work teams together, and clients to businesses. Love is also priceless—it doesn't have to cost a cent. The currency of love is our heart energy. We all have it and can tap into it if we open up.

The most amazing thing about love is that the more you give out by doing for others, the more you'll have left for yourself. Love is infinite. It has no limits. You'll never run out; love just keeps growing when you take action on it and give it away to other people.

Love Is a Verb

Love is something you do. It's the small and big things: the random acts of kindness, surprises, extra support, smiles, conversations, pats on the back, compliments, patience, kind thoughts, compassion, and many other acts of doing something for someone else.

Humans love touch. By reaching out and touching someone, holding hands, hugging, or giving someone a friendly pat on the back, hand, or shoulder, you will be lifting another person's spirit.

As Dr. Stephen Covey wrote in *The Seven Habits of Highly Effective People*, "next to physical survival, the greatest need of a human being is psychological survival - to be understood, to be affirmed, to be validated, to be appreciated." Therefore listening to other people—and speaking kind words to them and about them—is a loving gift that will satisfy their deepest needs.

Unconditional Love

Unconditional love means loving people regardless of their behavior or performance. It also means giving people the space to be who they are, without judgment. Having no limits or conditions to the love we give allows us to grow and break free of our own limiting patterns. Many feelings come up, and they must be felt and worked through. The process purifies both the giver and the receiver.

Loving unconditionally isn't easy. It requires living in the present moment, rejoicing, and receiving the gifts that are being presented when they appear—even if they don't feel wonderful at first.

Unconditional love is difficult to offer. It takes time and contemplation, going inside oneself, and asking a lot of questions. It has made me search for answers I didn't even know I had because they were buried under false beliefs of entitlement and high expectations. Unconditional love has required me to recognize the impatience that I feel, and push forward to find more patience. In a sense, I've had to become patient with my lack of patience and therefore a better giver, as well as more persistent and determined to offer and serve. Loving unconditionally has released me from thinking that I have to spend all my energy solving other people's issues or problems, because I love them with or without the issues. This has brought me more freedom in my heart, mind, time and energy.

Unconditional love has forced me to really look at *me* and the unreasonable expectations I have for myself and others; then I can rest in the discomfort of disappointment, feel my feelings, and examine how these expectations of myself and others do not serve my highest potential. In the period of resting in pain, disappointment, fear, anger, or loneliness, something emerges that is more beautiful than I ever could have imagined. A slight shift in someone else, an opening in myself, and an appreciation far beyond magnificent can appear in the smallest of happenings.

> *"When you love people, you have no time to judge them."*
> **—Mother Teresa**

People Need Connection

Never underestimate the power of spoken appreciation. What is a rekindled friendship worth to you? See how a simple act of appreciation reunited old friends in this story.

In the late 1970s, Jordan answered a classified ad to work part-time for a landscaping company in Illinois. Chuck, the owner of the company, hired him and taught him an extensive amount about being an entrepreneur. He also demonstrated the juggling act that was required to balance customer projects, finances (or lack thereof), employees, and equipment.

Jordan enjoyed working alongside Chuck, and it lit a spark inside him to start his own business one day. In the late '80s, the two went their separate ways.

About thirty-five years after he had first met Chuck, Jordan was taking his dream vehicle in for service at the Kachina Cadillac dealer in Scottsdale, Arizona. Lori, his service advisor, was very nice, did a first-class job, and always treated Jordan very well. After visiting the dealership every now and then for a year and a half, he had learned that Lori was leaving the dealership.

Jordan had just joined the company SendOutCards about two weeks prior, so he jumped on his computer to create a card to send to Lori. He uploaded a photo of himself standing in front of his truck and wrote a message to her: "Lori, I wish you the best in your career. I hope that our paths cross again soon, and I wanted to thank you for being such a tremendous service advisor for the past year and a half. Sincerely, Jordan." He included his phone number and sent the card.

Lori received the card, took it home, and set it on her kitchen counter.

About a week later, Jordan received a phone call. The gentleman on the other end of the line sounded familiar, but Jordan hadn't heard his voice in many years. The man didn't say his name. He just asked, "Do you know who this is?"

"Chuck?" Jordan said. He knew immediately but couldn't believe he had remembered his name after so many years, just from hearing his voice.

"Do you know a girl named Lori that works for Kachina Cadillac?" Chuck asked. "She's my wife."

"Just by sending a card to thank Lori," Jordan says, "I rekindled an old friendship. We now get together at least once a month. My first experience of being an entrepreneur with Chuck has come full circle. He and Lori have joined my organization and have just earned their promotion to manager."

> *"Kind words can be short and easy to speak,*
> *but their echoes are truly endless."*
> **—Mother Teresa**

We connect with people through our actions and words. Most of what is suggested here is free. It costs nothing to verbalize appreciation and praise. There could be a minor cost—such as writing a letter or sending a card or purchasing a small token of appreciation—but it's worthwhile investing in people and human connection.

Appreciation

After an encounter with someone, ask yourself whether you think that person feels better since meeting with you. If the answer is yes, you are making a difference.

Everyone has the power to positively influence the life of another by simply offering kind words of appreciation or acknowledgment. As a professional speaker, I'm often called upon to deliver eulogies at relatives' funerals. We come up with pages and pages of proof that the person who passed lived an honorable life, gave their time and support to teach lessons, and created lasting memories for others.

Why do we wait until someone dies before we pay tribute to who they were and appreciate them for their contributions and accomplishments? Why not pay tribute to someone living and give them compliments or recognize them for what they've done for you? You've got nothing to lose and everything to gain by writing or speaking words of appreciation and gratitude for others.

I vividly recall encouraging my brother Brian to share his appreciation for my Uncle Dennis while visiting him at the cancer hospice during his last days. Brian told me how Uncle Dennis had been such an important role model for him, and I said, "Tell him that." Well, that was easier said than done, but through an emotional voice, Brian shared from his heart with my uncle, and I was astounded at the healing I witnessed. My brother gave such beautiful words of recognition and appreciation, and my uncle soaked them up like a sponge. It's just as important to tell your family and close friends how much they mean to you as it is to be the one hearing it. Family ties hold a very significant place in our heart.

Families First

Kendra was four years old when her parents divorced. Often, over the next sixteen years, she wished she only had one family that could be all together. She loved both of her parents and step-parents and loved being a big sister to her three siblings, but she was the only tie between the two families.

Kendra struggled with feelings of guilt and thoughts of disappointing either side of her family. At times she wanted to do something with a friend but felt obligated to visit one of her families instead, as it was "their weekend." She often felt torn between the two sides, especially during holidays and special occasions. She felt she wasn't able to please everyone, and she blamed herself.

As she started to get older, Kendra found that her parents sometimes placed their differences on her. Sometimes her father would want her to meet at a certain time on a certain day, and her mother would want something different. Kendra was the messenger in the middle when one parent wanted something and the other didn't. "I think this is probably the hardest thing for any child to deal with. I think it is unfair to the child when they feel caught in the middle of their parents' disagreements," she says.

"We were an amicable family but still divided," Kendra says. "I always wished that the wall would come down between the two families. Kendra's mother asked her what she wanted to do to celebrate her nineteenth birthday. She told her mother she wanted to have a family dinner with all her parents and siblings at their home. "It was an easy answer," Kendra says. "It's all I've ever wanted, so I finally stood up for myself and spoke my truth."

Kendra's birthday wish came true. She and her mother invited Kendra's father's family to their home and enjoyed a family barbecue and cake. Her mother surprised everyone with a special gift for her daughter. She had her engagement ring and wedding band turned into a set of earrings and a pendant for Kendra. "The jewelry was amazing, and even more amazing was having one big, happy family. This was one of the greatest evenings of my entire life. When there is peace and harmony in the family unit, I feel whole," she says.

"Here's an excellent analogy. When you are divorced and there are children in the picture, treat it as a business relationship. Your ex-spouse is your business partner. In life, you don't always love the person you have to work with. Sometimes you really disagree with them, but for the sake of the business, you must communicate to make things work. Maybe you have negative feelings toward your ex. Remember they will always be Mom or Dad to your child. You and your ex have to come together no matter what the situation, and make things work as best as possible for your children. Put families first."

Kendra says she now feels empowered to be the link between her two families. "I have so much gratitude for everyone coming together to be one larger family for me," she says. "I love them all so much. It means the world to me that they all care about me enough to make things work out when necessary. I am honored and proud to say that I have an amazing blended family."

How Blended Are You?

A blended family is one that consists of two previously married parents and their children from those marriages, but from the perspective of a child, a blended family means that their two separate families blend. The marriage may be over, but the family isn't.

Regardless of the family structure you have, children are happiest when their home environments are peaceful. Clear, honest communication will help foster a peaceful environment. Be a role model in your family, whether you're the parent or the child, and take responsibility for making your relationships work.

What kind of gift will we give future generations if we can blend divided families and give more love and respect to all family members? Remember Kendra's story. Put your ego aside and act from the heart. After all, isn't love where the seeds of your family were planted?

Love in the Workplace

There is a workplace family too. From small companies to large corporations merging together, the same concept of blending relationships is critical for profitability and employee satisfaction. No matter the question, the answer is nestled somewhere in loving intention.

Is it proper to consider love and the workplace in the same thought? Absolutely. "Love" and "business" are two words you don't often hear in the same phrase, but the foundation of human needs exists whether we are at our professional place of business or in our personal place of living.

Love is key to success because solid business relationships are key to success. Loyal, strong relations are important to achieve success with your customers, employees, management, and the most import person—yourself.

How do you give love away in the workplace? More business-minded terms that represent love are respect, understanding, support, service, and having great intentions for others. Every day we deal with people, and people are creatures of emotion. Therefore, appealing to their emotional side and giving them what they want and need within the corporate boundaries demonstrates that you care. We succeed when we deeply care for others and invite them to have an interest in us and our services.

Love in a platonic sense totally suits the workplace. On the contrary, love affairs between coworkers are detrimental to the entire organization, and don't usually result in good business.

We may have originally thought that love and the workplace do not go hand in hand, yet love for oneself and others provides the basis for how we care for and about people. Isn't helping, serving, or benefiting people the key reason we got into business in the first place?

Build Mutually Supportive Relationships

Laurie had mastered the skills required as receptionist for a construction company, but she was bored. She asked her employer to find her something more mentally stimulating, and she recommended a friend to fill in as the firm's receptionist.

The company created a new position for Laurie to administrate a condominium complex project they had begun, and within a couple of years, when that job came to a close, she moved on once again.

"I always taught someone everything I knew about my positions while I was working within them," Laurie says. "I felt confident knowing that someone could step right in when I moved onward, and everything would continue to run smoothly. I never felt threatened by sharing my knowledge and information because I always believed that there was something or somewhere better for me in my career, even though I could not name it at the time. I avoided leaving tasks undone, to further ease new employees' transitions, and I always made sure someone was trained and capable of fulfilling my role."

Laurie's strategy of giving to others—sharing what she knew and giving herself aspiration for consistent growth on her career path—has evolved into her dream job. She's currently a successful entrepreneur, working from her beautiful country-set home, and making a living through giving, teaching others how to do the same, and changing the world.

> *"The best way to get promoted is to get*
> *your boss promoted and find your own replacement."*
> **—Unknown**

Cooperation Versus Competition

People in workplace environments don't always want to share their knowledge because they feel threatened. They feel that knowledge is power and that they become more powerful by withholding their knowledge. Nothing could be more detrimental to one's career.

Knowledge is not meant to be hoarded. Those who hoard do so under the false pretense that it makes them better leaders, but in reality they actually demonstrate a lack, a limitation, and a scarcity mentality, based on their fear that there isn't enough knowledge to go around for everyone.

> *"Cooperation, like love and friendship,*
> *is something you get by giving."*
> —Napoleon Hill

? How powerful will you be when you can share your information to build other leaders around you?
How vital will you be to your organization when you can coach people toward better skills and influence and inspire them to perform to the best of their abilities?

People are often stuck in dead-end careers because of their lack of ability to lead others. Don't hold back or keep secrets that could help someone else. You have experience to offer others. Teach it to them. You have resources others can use. Pass on that knowledge so others can benefit. Be the company's biggest cheerleader; encourage and empower others to grow. When one person wins, we all do. Always focus on cooperation versus competition in the workplace and beyond.

> *"Professionals create, amateurs compete."*
> —Bob Proctor

Be the Wind Beneath Their Wings

In his book *Beach Money: Creating Your Dream Life Through Network Marketing*, author Jordan Adler tells a story of how a single compliment affected his wealth. For many years, Jordan struggled in the network marketing industry. At one particular meeting, a senior-ranking distributor whom he did not know—but nevertheless recognized Jordan as someone who attended meetings regularly, sat in the front row, and introduced his guests to the speakers—handed him a slip of paper that read, "Nothing would make me happier than seeing you get your executive promotion."

"These simple words of encouragement were an investment in my inspiration," Jordan says. "It felt electrifying to be noticed, and I put away any doubt that I, too, could be a top income earner in the business."

From that day forward, Jordan began to work on his business with a renewed level of conviction and confidence and went on to earn a seven-figure income. He now devotes time every week to inspiring thousands of people in his organization.

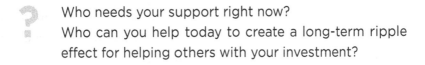

Who needs your support right now?
Who can you help today to create a long-term ripple effect for helping others with your investment?

Reach out to people and share what you have to give. A feeling of being supported and cheered for is often the wind beneath the wings of others and can develop their greatest potential.

Make an Investment in People

You may have the funds to offer or you may have less tangible gifts, perhaps words of encouragement or skills you can share, teach, or pass on in a mentoring role. This next example of someone investing in a student has paid dividends to a culture for many years.

The lights had dimmed in the Stratford Festival Theatre as Maurice made his way to his assigned seat for the play. He settled in then glanced at his armrest, where he saw an engraved brass plate bearing the name of a Festival sponsor. As his eyes focused to make out the writing, the hair on the back of his neck stood up. Professor John Pettigrew had sponsored the seat.

Back in 1965, Maurice had been one of fewer than 100 native students across Canada enrolled in post-secondary studies. At the start of his second year at Trent University, he decided to leave to take a job as a reporter at *The Intelligencer*, a daily newspaper in Belleville, Ontario. John Pettigrew, Maurice's English professor at Trent, had tried to coax him into continuing his studies and had even offered to pay his tuition if he stayed.

Although Maurice didn't accept the offer, he was amazed and honored that an almost complete stranger had that much confidence in him.

Several months prior, Maurice had accepted a generous offer of financial support from Dr. Gilbert Monture, a prominent citizen of Six Nations of the Grand River Mohawks. Dr. Monture had been made aware that, among Trent's initial 104 students, Maurice was the only one with First Nations heritage. His $400 gift covered the cost of a year's tuition, an amount equivalent to ten weeks' pay at the factory job Maurice had taken after completing high school and before enrolling in college.

"I am still humbled by these men's gestures of support for my future," Maurice says. "They had enough faith to invest in my ability to learn and to contribute to society. Even though both of these kind and generous guardian angels have passed on without me being able to express my thanks in person, it is never too late to show one's gratitude, and I like to think that I am showing my appreciation by contributing to the knowledge and understanding that Canadians have of First Nations peoples."

It makes Maurice proud that First Nations peoples, who have been his communications students and interns, are now working as professional journalists, lending their perspectives to news stories and informing thousands of readers and viewers. Indirectly, they are also repaying Professor Pettigrew and Dr. Monture.

A warm feeling enveloped Maurice as the play began. He experienced one of those fantastic moments that some people refer to as synchronicity—a sense that your life is on track.

"In the years ahead, I will feel twinges of that sentiment every time I attend plays at Stratford or drive through the scenic Trent campus straddling the Otonabee River just outside Peterborough," Maurice says.

"I will be reminded of the importance of supporting and encouraging others, and how fortunate I am that my life was touched by two men who already understood that lesson."

> *"No leader is self-made. Everyone was given a start by somebody else. That is a gift. Our gift back is to take responsibility and do our best to lead others with effectiveness and integrity."*
> **—John Maxwell**

Investing in people can be done anywhere—even in your favorite restaurant or at a tropical resort.

To Inspire Prompt Service

My fiancé, Dave, and I flopped into our lounge chairs, exhausted from the long journey from Canada and Puerto Vallarta. Our weeklong vacation at an all-inclusive resort was just getting started, so we'd have plenty of time to recharge our batteries following a busy work season and our hectic family life back at home.

I fell into a trance, gazing at the beautiful ocean, hearing the rhythm of the tide, and feeling the soft breeze on my face. *This is the life for me*, I thought.

Greeting us with a smile, a waitress walked by and offered to get us some drinks from the bar.

"*Dos* Coronas," Dave said and handed her a $20 tip.

"Holy mac," I remarked after the waitress left. "That was a huge tip for two drinks."

"Tips will inspire prompt service," he replied.

Boy, was Dave right. For the remainder of the week, the waitress found us no matter where we were. Not only did we receive prompt beverages, but we received blessings, greetings, humor, and even an education about life in that part of the world.

T.I.P.S. is an acronym that represents "To inspire prompt service." When you want to establish a dependable relationship and inspire expert service in a restaurant, put the tip on the table up front. When the server sees you're interested in their wellbeing, you'll have initiated a foundation for building a relationship, even for a short term.

Why not encourage the people serving you to perform at their best while you're experiencing their service rather than waiting until you've already been served? It's an investment that you'll benefit from during the service, rather than when it's over. You can give first and then enjoy receiving—receiving unconditionally of course, meaning allowing and honoring the best service someone knows how to give.

Give Back Time

Being self-employed, I keep a close watch on how I spend my time. Have you ever had days where you've been busy all day but you have no new beans to count? You know, those days when you haven't made a dime or feel like you've made any progress.

I call those days "give back time," when I give back to the abundant universe who gives to me. I do this by helping, volunteering, or sharing my knowledge via social media to those who follow me and my read my work.

I contemplate whether I've made a poor decision on how I've invested my precious time. I wonder whether I should have been more focused on making money, but in hindsight the people I help and serve—yet don't expect anything in return from—are often the ones who open up the greatest windows of earning opportunity for me down the road.

Service is about helping people. It's a form of loving in business.

Celebrate People

I asked Kody Bateman, CEO and founder of a multimillion dollar enterprise, to tell me a story about people celebrating other people. He told me about a famous author who celebrated him as a person.

Harvey Mackay, author of *Swim With the Sharks Without Being Eaten Alive*, attended one of Kody's seminars, and he spoke for a few minutes on stage. It was a wonderful experience, Kody says.

A few days later, Kody walked into his office and found a box on his desk with sharks all over it. There was no question where it had come from. He opened the box and found a personal letter, along with all six of the books Mackay had written, as well as an invitation for Kody to be included in a project that Mackay was working on.

"I will follow Harvey Mackay to the end of the world because of that package," Kody says. "He is a big-time famous guy, and I am an up-and-comer, and yet he celebrated me. He treated me like I was the king of a land somewhere. He gave me a sense of respect. I want to make everyone I meet feel that they are the most important person in the world at the moment of our meeting."

Meeting and establishing a relationship with someone famous or living a life that you idolize is a great way to increase your self-worth. It's not impossible to meet your heroes. Just start by giving.

The Power of the Written Word

Sharon is a young professional who mustered up the courage to approach Lynn Johnston, the creator of the syndicated comic strip *For Better or For Worse*.

"We were at a fundraising event," remembers Sharon, "and I just really wanted to get to know her as a person. I approached her with a compliment on her amazing contribution of wit, humor, and art that she has made to society."

A few days later, Sharon followed up with Lynn by asking for a lunch meeting, and Lynn agreed. Her intention was only to learn more about her.

"Tell me of your journey," Sharon said and listened. "When did you begin to encounter the fame that you have today?" Sharon asked and listened. "You are truly an inspiration," Sharon complimented and affirmed. "If you ever need any of my services," she said, "Feel free to ask of me."

"We had a lovely lunch at a local diner, talking and laughing as if we weren't new acquaintances but true friends," Sharon says. "What I remember most of our conversation was how appreciative she was that I didn't ask her for anything. As you can imagine, most people of significant nature and stature are constantly hounded for this and that. My intention was only to give, to appreciate, and to validate Lynn."

That evening, Sharon handwrote a thank-you card, appreciating Lynn for the time she had spent with her over lunch, her shared wisdom, and her contributions to the community, and dropped it into the mail. Two weeks later she received a handwritten letter back from Lynn. "Dear Sharon," it read, "I was impressed to receive a novel handwritten card from you, an art that is rare these days, yet still being practiced by a young person."

Since then, Sharon and Lynn have continued to keep in touch via snail mail. "This relationship has enriched my life by knowing that famous people are real people, and I too am real, with a whole lot of potential," says Sharon.

Listening and giving appreciation and validation are the strike that can spark anyone's spirit. Mother Nature demonstrates this for us in the animal kingdom, and it operates in the workplace just as nicely.

Teamwork—Honk if You're Happy

One amazing example of cheering each other on in the animal kingdom is that of Canada geese. Together, flying in a "V" formation, flocks of Canada geese cover amazing distances—up to 1,000 miles per day—and you can certainly hear them coming and going as they fly overhead. While flying in formation, the geese honk to encourage those up front to keep up their speed. They cheer on their leader, and when the leader gets tired, it moves to the back and another goose takes over. The previous leader cheers from the back.

The Power of the Spoken Word

We all "honk" in one way or another at work, but is our honking encouraging? When encouragement is part of a group's culture, production is much higher and individuals feel empowered as a result of good-quality "honking."

Praise your coworkers' efforts in a descriptive way. For example, you might say, "Joan, your new account has brought an abundance of activity to the shipping department. We're thankful to have so many orders to fill." Compliment and encourage others, and watch your work culture take flight toward your goals with speed, accuracy, and distance.

Giving and receiving praise are equally satisfying. Don't wait for someone else to give you the praise you've been waiting for. Start dishing it out. As the boomerang effect suggests, "If you want it to come back, first you have to throw it."

Saying nothing is not a good option. The absence of praise makes neutral statements seem negative, because neutral statements possess no fuel for boosting confidence or building self-esteem.

Praising Everyone Is Counterproductive

Early in my direct sales career, I was called onto a stage to be recognized for achieving sales challenges I hadn't even met. The company was fairly new, and the staff wanted to motivate conference attendees and recognize their performance and achievement. Although I hadn't yet met their benchmark, they recognized me as if I had anyway, with a decorative award and engraved plaque.

After the ceremony, I asked the management why they had recognized me despite my lack of achievements. They said they wanted my team to respect me as an accomplished leader. Well, it was an interesting show for my team, but I couldn't display the awards without a feeling of failure, so I kept them in boxes, tucked away so they wouldn't remind me of my undeserved success. He who compliments everyone compliments no one.

A friend of mine told me about his eight-year-old daughter's hockey season. She has about eight trophies and medals after only two years of play, yet she rarely even touched the puck. What message do we send our children about achievement when they're recognized for accomplishments that don't even exist?

In the late 1960s, teachers were influenced to remove anything potentially damaging to self-esteem from their curriculums, because esteem is the most important facet of a person.[5] Soccer coaches stopped counting goals and gave trophies to all players; teachers threw away their red pens; criticism was replaced with undeserved praise. This hasn't served us.

As in the case of the hockey trophy collector who rarely touched the puck, we must be careful when giving praise to avoid de-motivating someone from continuous effort. For example, telling someone they're doing a good job could prevent them from striving to do better. Telling a schoolchild they're smart can frustrate them when they aren't feeling or performing as "smart" as they typically do.

Intelligence is not innate; it must be developed. Rather than telling people, that they're smart or good, praise them for their *efforts*. When you do so, they'll work harder to develop their natural gifts. Leaders, teachers, managers, coaches, and parents who offer undeserved praise may send the message that their pupils have reached the limit of their innate abilities, while those who offer constructive feedback convey a message that the pupils can improve their performance even more.

---

5   Nathaniel Branden -1969 publication of *The Psychology of Self-Esteem*

With intermittent reinforcement, the brain learns that frustrating spells can be worked through. If a person grows used to being rewarded too frequently, he or she may lack persistence through the tougher times when rewards are scarce.

Just how do we offer criticism in a productive way?

The Right Way to Praise

You can counter these problems with descriptive praise, which describes how you see or feel things. In the three previous examples (complimenting someone on a *great* meal, praising a coworker for dressing *nicely*, and commending a golfer on his or her *good* shot), I used italics to demonstrate praise using words that evaluate—*great*, *nicely*, and *skillful*.

Rather than using evaluating words, tell someone what you **see** or **feel** when your intention is to praise them:

"I see you have excellent experience in the kitchen and can make a meal fit for a king."

"I feel more alive when you enter the room with that brilliantly colored shirt and matching tie. It seems to me that you are always so well-dressed."

"I witnessed a beautiful golf swing on your first tee, Ryan."

If you really look, listen, and experience what someone is doing for you, stating out loud what you see and feel goes into the person's emotional bank account and cannot be taken away.

If you merely say "Good job" or "Good boy," it can easily be erased the very next day with "Bad job" or "Bad boy," but descriptive praise such as "I see you've completed the task on time and with amazing accuracy" becomes an affirming touchstone in someone's life, one that cannot be erased and sets a new benchmark for continued and greater success.

"The deepest principle in human nature
is the craving for appreciation."
—William James

Resisting Praise

There are several inherent problems with praise. Let's take a look at them.

Doubt: Some people doubt the praise they receive. Let's say someone compliments you on a *great* meal that you feel was mediocre. If you're not allowing it to land, you may feel they're just trying to appease you. ("If they think that was delicious, they must be lying."), or perhaps you think the compliment has manipulative intentions ("He's trying to butter me up.").

Denial: Sometimes praise can lead to immediate denial. Perhaps you've praised someone in your office for their ability to dress so *nicely* all the time. They may immediately develop sensitivity to how poorly dressed they are on weekends. Praise can also feel threatening. ("How will I dress for the next business meeting?")

Negative focus: Praise can encourage one to focus on their weaknesses. A typically terrible golfer who makes a *skillful* first shot is praised for their command of the game. This praise, however, might make them feel a tremendous amount of anxiety to continue to perform at this caliber.

The Power of Praise, Recognition, and Acknowledgment

*"A pat on the back is just a few vertebrae up
from a kick in the pants but is miles ahead in results."*
—Ella Wheeler Wilcox

Maya Angelou said, "I've learned that people will forget what you said, people will forget what you did, but people will never forget how you made them feel" —Whether you made them feel good or bad, people remember their feelings over the message, or lesson, or service that you gave them. There's humongous power in giving others affirmation. Praise, recognition, and acknowledgment help others feel self-value.

Whose Role Is It Anyway?

In the workplace, people think praise should come from the top; in other words, praise is the role of management. I disagree. It's everyone's responsibility to contribute toward creating the corporate culture in which they want to work. This is no different in families or any relationships. For a positive culture, you've got to first be positive. Part of being positive is sharing gratitude for all that's in your life or workplace. We often overlook what is and instead think and talk about what isn't.

The next time you walk into your place of employment or your home, count 100 things you are thankful for, and then verbalize some of your gratitude toward the people who created these things. "I am thankful for this security system that I must pass through because it keeps me safe. I am thankful for clean hallways and lights to guide me in. I am thankful for the shoes, coats, and toys all over the floor, because I know my kids are home." Can you think of ninety-seven more?

Be A Strength Seeker

Don't be a fault finder, instead be a strength seeker. Be the one who notices your fellow employees, friends, or family members doing things right, and speak to them about it. Verbally catching people doing things right versus wrong will give them the feeling of pride which will always stay with them. You'll contribute to a very positive corporate or family culture—one in which you and others will want to work and thrive.

> *"Your team members are the co-creators*
> *of your dreams and aspirations."*
> **—Napoleon Hill**

The Compliment Jar

A simple glass jar and slips of paper gave Edie's dental office team contagious enthusiasm. "We labeled it our 'Compliment Jar' and placed it in our lunch room," Edie explains. "We inspired the team to 'catch people doing things right' by filling out a deposit slip to record who did something well and what they did for our patients or the team."

During the office's morning team huddle, they'd read the entries. One that had particular impact recognized their dentist, who had helped a family who was going through a difficult financial time. One of their children needed treatment, and the dentist provided the service free of charge.

"The impact it had on our team was really powerful," says Edie. "It was a very humbling experience for all of us. The act of kindness really touched our hearts. When we read the deposit slip, our dentist was surprised too that it had such an impact on the family he helped and the entire dental team who represented him. Pride from giving the gift of service energized us to give more of ourselves. As a team, we know what each member does, but when someone takes the time to write down how you have gone above and beyond, it boosts confidence and morale. Making a difference in the office in a positive way will keep everyone looking for the good in each other."

Make time to do something that packs so much motivation into a few minutes with your team or family. It's fun and free, and it will bring you closer to that fuzzy feeling.

The Emotional Currencies of Secure Relationships

The metaphor about an emotional bank account to demonstrate relationship strategies between people was introduced by Stephen Covey. Inside each of us is an emotional vault. Love, support, praise, recognition, and acknowledgment make us feel secure when deposited into our emotional bank accounts, just as money deposited into our financial bank accounts contributes to our financial security. Withdrawals from our emotional bank accounts are also a part of life. We need to communicate corrections, reprimands, constructive feedback, and things that might not necessarily be well received by their recipients.

The key to mutually beneficial and healthy relationships is to ensure you are making more deposits than withdrawals the emotional bank accounts of those with whom you want to have strong relationships. Take note of what you offer in the way of words.

Are you a constant fault-finder and naysayer, always communicating what is wrong or inadequate? Or do you usually offer words that make people feel valued and validated, with occasional constructive feedback?

The worst that can happen to an emotional bank account is that we go bankrupt, meaning we've withdrawn more than we've deposited. Bankrupt relationships can be brought back to a positive balance with consistent deposits of love, support, recognition and acknowledgement. In this instance, keep giving.

We all want to have relationships with an abundant emotional bank account; therefore, we need a healthy balance of more deposits than withdrawals.

Give to Others and Receive the Benefits

Use the strategies of giving to others in this chapter to help build a wealth of positive emotions within your family and your workplace. If you do so, your emotional bank accounts, and those of the people closest to you, will always feel secure with an abundant balance.

The people in our lives are a precious gift, loaned to us only temporarily. Don't wait to tell them how important they are and how grateful you are to have them in your life while you can still celebrate them. If you *aspire* to *inspire* before you *retire* or *expire*, you'll be able to give love and build joyful relationships.

Unconditionally loving someone means having desires but not being attached to the outcome; rather we must allow things to unfold and feel compassion for the hearts involved. Giving from the heart to others nurtures us deeply with appreciation and knowingness that when the slightest sign or gift is offered back to us it is pure, not enforced, and without strings attached. It also hasn't been given out of obligation or expectations, thus allowing us to receive from our highest selves.

Some of us die with a lot of money, assets, and stuff. Have you ever seen a hearse pulling a U-Haul? You can't take it with you, so why not share some of what you have with others while you're alive and experience the riches of watching people benefit from your gifts? So much of the world relies on charitable service and donations, which is the topic of the next chapter.

If you ask a person on their deathbed what they wish for, they likely will tell you they want love, peace, and joy, or more time to create these feelings with those who are important in their lives. Celebrate people now. Don't hold back. Don't wait. You may not have another chance. In giving to others, we grow rich in ways that we never could have imagined possible.

 Giving to Charity

*"One of the most difficult things to give away
is kindness—it is usually returned."*
—C. Flint

My son and I were at Canadian Tire, one of Canada's largest retailers, picking out a basketball net when I bumped into a shining star in our community.

"Scott Clark," I greeted him enthusiastically, hoping he might share with me a story about the concept of giving and growing rich.

"Hello, Penny! How are things with you?" replied Scott, his voice cheery as always.

"Super. I'm writing a book and looking for stories and examples from exemplary givers like you. Can you tell me about a time when you gave something and it had a major effect on people's lives?"

Scott recalled his story as though it had happened yesterday. It started with a motorcycle ride and a conversation with Steve Haws of the local Rotary Club about a Northern Ontario camp for disabled children being closed down due to lack of funding.

With Scott's experience as a morning radio show host, he and Steve discussed the potential of a radio-thon. After a week of deliberation and researching the Guinness World Records, they decided to host "The Longest Morning Show Ever" in an effort to raise money for Rotary for Kids, a charity that supports disabled children and families who rely on these funds to provide better lives for their children.

Their goal was to raise $20,000, and despite the criticism they received from many people telling them it wouldn't work, they were successful. "I learned that there are about five world records that people constantly try to break, and radio hosts staying awake as long as they can was one of them," Scott told me. "Often doctors were needed, people collapsed, and stimulants other than coffee were used, but for the sake of my health, we would solicit the help of others in the community."

When they started the radio-thon, they began telling stories. Students from Canadore College came on board to help them interview families to get their stories, and the radio station replayed their stories on air. "We heard stories about what life is like having a child with a disability; the long and lonely hours that families would travel to get the specialty care that these children needed; what it was like to get their children fitted for prosthetics," Scott said. "It really resonated with the community. The stories were like magic. All the planets aligned."

During the three-day radio-thon, Scott and his crew raised more than $50,000 and purchased a wheelchair lift for a family who never could have afforded it. Their son had grown and the family could no longer pick him up out of his wheelchair and carry him up their stairs to his bedroom. The family received a lift that would help get him to his room. Just knowing that their boy no longer had to spend his nights sleeping in the family's dining room was an incredible feeling for Scott and everyone involved.

"I gave time and effort," Scott told me, "but there were so many others who gave their time, effort and money, connected with the people here, and bought things locally for their children; and there are probably thousands of stories and thousands of lives improved because of the community donations."

"Wow, what a praiseworthy story, Scott." I said, grateful for his contribution to my book, and impressed with the amount of money that can be raised when people get creative and work toward a common cause. "How did you get rich in that experience?" I asked him.

"The legacy lives on," Scott stated with pride. "The same fundraiser continues without me. This year they raised $100,000 for the cause. Over a million dollars has been raised in this community since that first radio-thon. But there is one other story that came out of that same fifty-two-hour marathon," he continued, "and of all the stories that I have from my days in radio, this is my favorite story."

Scott proceeded to tell me that Randy Bachman, the Canadian musician and lead guitarist and songwriter of The Guess Who, happened to be in town that weekend and heard about the radio-thon. Randy has a grandchild who has special needs, so he called and said he wanted to pop into the show. He dropped by the station with a bunch of signed memorabilia, and the radio station was able to auction items off to help support the cause.

"I said to my co-host at the time, Catherine Murphy, 'This is super cool. We've got to get him to sign something for us,' " Scott told me. "So Catherine ran home for an old guitar that she kept under her bed. It was all beat up and missing a string."

During his time on the air, Randy Bachman told stories, connected with the audience, and gave a terrific interview, but Scott's favorite radio moment of all time occurred when he asked Randy to play something.

"Well, I don't have my guitar," Randy said.

"Here's one," Catherine offered, and handed him her guitar.

Randy sat there tuning that old guitar and telling Scott and Catherine about a concert he performed at many years ago. "He said that after the concert, he tried to figure out a certain piece of music, and—wouldn't you know it—he played the iconic start to 'American Woman' on this crappy old guitar in our studio and told us how that song came about," Scott told me. "It sounded as fresh as anything you have ever heard, and that moment I was sitting there with this incredible music icon and goose bumps."

Scott smiled and added "What would it cost to have Randy Bachman sit at your kitchen table to play you 'American Woman'? That was the enrichment I received—my most spectacular radio moment and raising money for kids at the same time in the longest morning show ever."

> *"Service to others is the rent*
> *you pay for your room here on earth."*
> —**Muhammad Ali**

A World of Difference

Without the donation of millions of dollars annually, and service by volunteers to worthwhile programs, our communities would not be able to exist. Health, world peace, saving the planet, feeding the hungry, housing the homeless—these are all real needs of real people who reap the benefits of financial donations and contributions of people's time. In the giving of either, the giver is privileged to experience in unimaginable ways, just like Scott's best radio moment memory with Randy Bachman.

Find a cause you truly believe in and give to it. The benefits of giving far outweigh the investment associated, and you'll be content knowing you're making a world of difference.

Any Amount Makes a Big Difference

While attending a fiftieth birthday party for a girlfriend, I learned that in lieu of gifts she was asking for donations to La Tienda, a fair trade art co-op that serves a group of women and their families in the Dominican Republic. The women of La Tienda make beautiful jewelry, fabric, and handmade artwork to sell in order to be independent and provide for their children.

I was moved to hear of the challenges these women face and the efforts of this co-op to educate and empower them to take responsibility for their lives and support themselves and their families. After the party, I mailed in a financial contribution.

I was interested in interviewing the program coordinator, Raquel Stricklee, for this book, about her personal mission. During the interview, I mentioned that my small contribution was most likely a drop in the bucket for her cause.

"No, Penny," she replied, "your contribution was a large chunk of what we needed to build our storage room, a secure area to store supplies and items for sale. Now the materials and finished products that the women make are kept secured and are safe from thieves."

After realizing how far my dollars could go to help the thirty families that belong to this co-op, I was motivated to continue giving. When I'm shopping, I often put down an item that I would have previously bought, realizing that the $10 or $20 it costs could be better spent by giving it away to a charitable cause—one that helps build skills toward a better future for women and their families. Any amount you can give makes a big difference.

"Give what you have; to someone it may
be better than you dare to think."
—Henry Wadsworth Longfellow

You can offer money, time, talent—or even a bike!—and make a world of difference. David was the recipient of the Scotia Thompson Award, a public recognition for someone who has made a difference. His contribution was with the Seventh Generation First Nations charity, to which he had donated his time for many years. This year, he simply bought a bike for a child. The recipient, a young boy, had saved up his money and purchased a bike all by himself. His father had warned him not to leave it outside, for fear it might get stolen. The boy, however, didn't listen to his father, and the next day he discovered the bike had been stolen. At the recognition event for David, the boy and his family came over to meet him.

"I had never been recognized for donating to charity," David says. "I preferred to give in secret, yet seeing what my gift had meant to that boy brought me a joy I will never forget. I could see the joy in his face as our eyes met at the event."

As the boy hugged David in thanks, he told the boy, "I want you to know that there are nice people in the world too and that you should listen to your dad."

"I knew that this simple financial contribution to buy a kid a bike could have influenced how he lived the rest of his life," David says. "Giving to young people can have a lifelong impact on them, with a ripple effect that extends far across countries, lifetimes, and societal barriers."

This bike, like any other offering for a child, whether it be new or gently used, can pedal their hearts forward in the direction of feeling secure, and knowing that the world is a safe and fertile place for opportunity.

The opportunity to give is everywhere.

I sat in my dentist's chair, and marveled at a story he told me about generous giving that has extended through multiple generations.

Dennis was renovating his dental office and had to get rid of equipment, furniture, cabinetry, and a computer system. It seemed a shame to toss the items into a landfill, but he didn't know who to give them to or what to do with them.

About two weeks prior to the scheduled renovation, Dennis and his wife Nadine were invited to a cocktail party by a gentleman they had met at a fundraising event for the Toronto East General Hospital, one of the charities the couple supported. The function was hosted by the French Council General for Canada at an outdoor venue at York University to celebrate France's Independence Day.

A well-dressed boy, about five or six years old, stole their attention with his eloquent manners. After watching him for a while, Dennis and Nadine approached his parents to compliment them on their child's behavior. They learned that the boy's parents, Jean-Michel and Mariat, were representatives for the Republic of the Congo in Africa.

"What do you do for a living?" Mariat asked Dennis.

"I'm a dentist," he replied.

"I'm trying to start a dental clinic for an orphanage in the Republic of the Congo," she said. "Can you help me?"

"What are you doing Monday?" Dennis smiled and invited her to visit his dental practice to view the equipment he no longer needed. "In about two weeks, I'm renovating my office, and I can donate everything and anything you want to use."

Mariat was almost in tears of joy. She had been struggling to find equipment for her orphanage dental clinic and had found Dennis.

"It was a gratifying feeling—knowing, as we left the party, that we could donate our old dental office to a good cause," Dennis says. "Of the 300 attendees, we were drawn to the ones who needed us the most. Our history of giving resulted in an invitation to this event, and in accepting and attending, we were able to connect with one more cause."

The following Monday, Mariat and her husband came to the office. "We'll take it all!" she exclaimed.

"I'm not sure if the electricity and computer system will work for you as it has here in Canada," Dennis cautioned.

"Not only will this help the orphanage with a new dental clinic," Mariat said, "but it will help educate people in assembling it and making it function. It will also occupy people to rebuild and modify the cabinets, electrical work, and anything else that needs to be done."

During the renovation, Jean-Michel and Mariat showed up with a crew and a truck and loaded up everything the clinic had to give—even the light bulbs!

The second leg of the journey to erect a dental clinic in the Republic of the Congo involved shipping the cargo. As a member of the East York Kiwanis Association—and a former president of the association and a Mel Osborne Fellow—Dennis made some phone calls to different Kiwanis organizations that reach out around the world. Their motto is "Children Priority One."

As Dennis and his friends searched for the financial resources to ship the items overseas, they determined that the underserviced area where the orphanage was located didn't have a Kiwanis organization nearby. They had a connection through UNICEF and pulled every string to find assistance for shipping, only to be met with budgetary restraints that didn't allow funding for the container of goods to be shipped by air or water.

Dennis put the Congo representatives in touch with their connections, hoping that the political people of the world could help them get the products to their destination. Though they tried to find one person who had the ability to authorize or fund a delivery, they were only able to leave it in the hands of the service organizations to get it delivered.

Service Clubs

Dennis had gotten his children involved in Kiwanis when they were in middle school. "We helped start a Builders' Club, a service club for kids in grades six through eight," he says. "This club has grown to over fifty students of various ethnic backgrounds, all of whom are self-governing, fundraising machines. In doing so, they are developing social skills that many kids just don't have."

From this, a KEY Club was formed at Marc Garneau Collegiate Institute in East York, Toronto. This club is now the largest Key Club in Canada, involving 120 to 130 high school students from various ethnic backgrounds in Thorncliffe Park, a very needy area of Toronto. The club invites the kids to Kiwanis meetings, and they experience the organization's protocol and structure. The children say a Kiwanis grace, sing the national anthem, and toast the Queen.

"The kids come for the first time and giggle, but the second time they show up in shirts and ties and know what fork to use to eat their dinner," Dennis says. "It really teaches them skills beyond fundraising. The benefits of giving and social conscience teaches adults and kids about responsibility, proper manners, protocol, and respect, all of which go beyond selling a hot dog for a dollar and passing the money on to charity."

Fellow dentists often ask Dennis why he gives his time to serve organizations and how he finds time to help in these ways. "I do it because that is the way we were brought up. My parents were factory workers. We didn't have a lot of money, so all we had to give was our time," he explains.

Dennis raised his children based on this experience. He and Nadine told them they didn't have to worry about making a living when they were adults, or getting the best marks in school, or going to the best colleges. They only asked them to focus on how they could give to others, in service, with their unique talents. "You have a unique talent that no one else on earth has, and a special way of expressing that talent to serve others," they often told their children.

"In teaching our children this way, they have become considerate givers," Dennis says. "They got excellent grades in school, went to the best universities, and became financially self-sufficient because they were focused on what they were here on earth to give."

Dennis and Nadine's son has been involved with Kiwanis and just started a club at the University of Toronto's Scarborough campus. Their daughter is in involved with Kids Help Phone, a helpline that children and teenagers in Canada can call for assistance and advice twenty-four hours a day, 365 day a year.

"Who wouldn't want this for their children?" Dennis says. "There is so much satisfaction in knowing that you helped someone somewhere. Giving makes you feel good and increases self-worth."

Meeting genuine, honest people has been a huge benefit for Dennis, and he's grateful for those he meets and reconnects with through his efforts to give. "I would be lying if I said that it does not impact my dental practice in a very positive way," he says. "Anyone on any of the boards or service organizations that I sit on refers me as a dentist and TMD/orthodontic specialist because I am always on their mind."

Receiving back from the process of giving is more than okay. It's necessary, because it completes the circle of abundance.

> *"Give, and it will be given to you. A good measure,*
> *pressed down, shaken together, and running over,*
> *will be poured into your lap. For with the measure*
> *you use, it will be measured to you."*
> **—Luke 6:38**

? Do you have time to give to a service club in your community?
Do you have items you can donate to help others in need?
Do you think you are too young or too old to get started on the journey of giving?

The Apple Doesn't Fall Far from the Tree

This proverb means that kids grow up to be like their parents. Giving has a snowball effect in families where parents or children set an example and the whole family jumps on the bandwagon.

As a single mom raising five children, Ellen recognized the needs that so many families have in our communities, so she volunteered her spare time at a local food bank. Ellen's son, Cal, came along with her to help out. During his own physical healing, and while serving others less fortunate that him, he was inspired to help all children have a happier birthday, regardless of their situation.

In 2006, at age eleven, Cal founded his first program. He created Cal's Club, which provides birthday packages—including cake mix, icing, and age-appropriate toys—for needy children. Although they didn't really keep track of the numbers of packages distributed in the early years, as of 2011, Cal has provided more than 1,500 of these birthday packages to the North Bay, Callander, and Powassan Food Banks, Low Income People Involvement, the Transition House, the Indian Friendship Centre, and other agencies that serve families in need.

Cal didn't stop there. In 2010 he launched the "Walk-a-Mile" program. While volunteering at the food bank, he saw a number of children come in with substandard footwear, or in some cases none at all. In August of that same year he collected and donated 113 pairs of top-quality shoes to needy kids. Cal also has given in a number of other ways, such as providing bags of cosmetics to women on Mother's Day at the food bank. Cal's Club also offers a community service award each year to a deserving eighth grade graduate who has demonstrated an exemplary commitment to community service.

With a long list of provincial and national service awards, Cal continues his family's tradition of community service; every one of his siblings has become involved in improving the lives of those in their respective communities.

"Through what initially was inspired by meeting the needs of kids' birthdays with the love of giving gifts and making people happy," Ellen says, "Cal discovered that helping others was a way to take his mind off his own troubles. He was seriously ill for a long time, and Cal's Club allowed him to focus on others without thinking of the sports, school, and activities that he was missing."

Cal has never been held back by convention or age. He has always been a free-range kind of kid who likes to try new things, whether or not others might see them as doable.

"Starting this club was a challenge for him. As a family, we really encouraged it," says Ellen. "Cal's Club has given Cal an opportunity to examine various career paths. He's had the chance to run a 'business' and examine social justice issues. His plan is to pursue a career in poverty law."

Starting at age eleven, this boy found a need, filled it, and continues to make a difference. If this isn't a shining example of an exemplary giver who is rich with experience and awareness of life's potential, I don't know what is.

It's never too early or late in life to make a difference. Begin today by giving in your own community. Cal does, and so can you. Giving can be performed through time and service, or have a monetary value. Some of the greatest financial gurus state that tithing is one of the keys to acquiring massive wealth.

Tithing

A spiritual teacher cooked a meal for his large group. As he passed out servings, it became clear that some who had received food at the beginning of the serving were given larger portions and some near the end got nothing at all. Those with plenty shared with those without, and the lesson of tithing was revealed. We are all connected in the chain of giving, and when we are awake to the needs of others, we can be a responsible channel for the universe to flow through. By tithing, we honor the nature of our generous heart, which is to be both receiving and giving.

Tithing is a principle of giving a portion of your earnings to those in need, not necessarily as a charitable act, but more so as an obligation. To put it into perspective, a tithe is a recognition of those who have contributed to your success, and when it is paid, you honor your place in the circle of abundance. You are not the source, nor the stopping point, of the riches; rather you are in the middle. Allowing some of your riches to flow out assures that you stay in the middle.

John Templeton, one of the world's champion financial advisors, once was asked, "What is the best advice ever given to people in regard to their finances?" He answered, "Tithing. I have never known anyone who has tithed for ten years and has not had it come back tenfold."

You do not need to have a lot of money to make a difference in the world by tithing. Different people have different percentages. One common suggestion is to offer 10 percent to a charitable cause and 10 percent to your savings account, then live off the other 80 percent of your income.

Having money flow through us is an amazing feeling.

Thirteen Thank-Yous

The families of thirteen patients assembled in preparation for Family Day, a monthly event scheduled for parents, siblings, and spouses to visit their loved ones who had found the need to begin their journey toward recovering from their illnesses.

"Before we begin, we'd like to thank one of our parents here today for the generous donation that she gave to our program," said one of the patients.

I was handed a greeting card. Later that day, I opened the card. Inside were thirteen handwritten mini-paragraphs of appreciation and gratitude from each and every person in the program, thanking me for making possible the purchase of a new PlayStation 2 for their lounge. The patients spend most of their waking hours in this room, and the supplies and items that occupy their time are purchased through fundraising and donations.

The patients wrote messages such as "We are touched and grateful for your generous and thoughtful contribution to the welfare of our community."; "Thank you. We are all very excited!"; "Thank you so much for your generosity and kindness."; "From the bottom of my heart I want to thank you, not just for the donation, but also for being such an inspiration."; "More people should be like you—a true heart with genuine care and compassion."; and "Thank you for restoring my faith in mankind."

I was able to channel funds into this important cause by using my talents as a speaker and requesting a donation to this charity in exchange for a keynote speech I gave. It felt incredible to give my time to serve an audience, and then, with donating the funds I earned to another cause, to change thirteen more lives, and many more in the future. I'll always remember this feeling, but I would have long forgotten the deposit of funds into my own bank account or the stuff I would have spent the money on.

No amount of money kept to oneself can buy this feeling of making a contribution. We all possess the ability to reach out and give to others, whether our gift is money, material items, words of encouragement, a greeting card, a smile, a prayer, or a compliment. Giving to others gives us a powerful sense of joy.

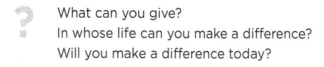

What can you give?
In whose life can you make a difference?
Will you make a difference today?

By reaching out and offering something to someone, you may or may not receive thirteen thank-yous, but you will be blessed with an internal sense of joy that no amount of money can buy.

"Too many people spend money to buy things
they don't want to impress people they don't like."
—Unknown

The Joy Junkie

Giving to charitable causes circulates abundant wealth and changes lives. Some people make time for giving on missions by using their vacation or a leave of absence from the office.

In 2007, when Nick was twenty-seven, he spent three weeks in Hawaii living the life of an extreme adventurer. Surfing, skydiving, zip lining, flying glider planes, swimming with sharks, scuba diving, and mountain climbing were many of the tangible experiences he had received and enjoyed during his vacation.

Shortly after Nick returned home to Columbus, Ohio, he left for a mission with his church, which he had paid for six months prior. His destination was Haiti. "I was terrified of leaving my world behind, of going completely 'dark,'" Nick admits. "This meant turning off my cell phone and not having access to email or text messages. I feared that my real estate business would die while I was gone and that I would be broke by the time I came back."

From the paradise of Hawaii to the dire conditions in Haiti, Nick's life changed completely. The heat was extreme; the confusion of the airport, with so many people yelling, pushing and aggressively seeking money and support felt overwhelming.

Nick set off on a bus and looked out the window at the worst poverty he had ever seen. There was garbage everywhere, burning trash, naked children; what he saw made him not even want to look. Nick felt guilty knowing he had so much and these people had so little. "Most of the world lives in poverty," he says. "Most of the world does not live like North Americans do, and the saddest part was not that the Haitians have so little but that we have so much."

Over a short time, Nick fell in love with the Haitians but hated their situation. He started to feel that he had found his purpose, the reason for his life. "I remember my satisfaction in the manual labor," he says, "working with a shovel and dirt yet being so filled with joy knowing that I was doing God's will. We built a house of concrete blocks, dedicated it to a family, and handed out clothes, shoes, and starter packages for new mothers who had just had babies. With each gift we gave, we would pray with the recipients for a while."

Eight or nine hours of hauling forty-pound cinder blocks was something Nick never would have done back home; instead he'd hire someone to do it for him. In this instance, however, providing this service to others gave him a joy he had never felt before. "Rather than the material greatness that I received in Hawaii, I preferred the feeling of giving in service to others," he says. "I have learned that giving has nothing to do with gain. It's done simply for the love and joy that I get from doing God's will."

In his early thirties, Nick has learned at a young age what is truly important. As a result, he realizes he has the capacity to do even more. "I'm a joy junkie!" he says. "Working to help others gives me the richness of feeling joy. I am addicted to serving people and prefer missions to Haiti over vacations in Hawaii, where I can serve my purpose."

After his time in Haiti, Nick returned to Ohio with a new motivation to grow his business even more so he could give more to others. After three years of prayer and asking how he could do more than just visit Haiti and build a house or hand out clothes or food, he met a Canadian missionary named Tony Jones who was exporting coffee.

MoreThanCoffee.org purchases coffee directly from Christian farmers and missionaries to create sustainable employment on the farms on which the coffee is grown. Profits from the sales of the coffee fund other missions so they can provide food, education, clean water, and medical care, and also build churches, schools, and homes for people in need.

Tony uses the proceeds from MoreThanCoffee.org to fund five schools, a literacy program to teach people how to read, and a feeding program for kids and adults in Haiti, and Nick decided to help.

"God sends people to me when I need them to fill in any gaps that I have," Nick says. "I was introduced to a fellow Christian, Graham Robinson of Northern Computer Services, who offered to do our websites, programming, and e-commerce, and Jos, who runs our MoreThanCoffee.ca site to sell coffee in Canada."

Nick stayed at Tony's home in Haiti while he helped him work. It was so hot that he sweated through both sides of his pillow. For two weeks, Nick asked if he could buy a fan from the market to cool the home slightly, but Tony told him if he did that, he would have to look at the fan every day and be reminded of how many people he could have fed for the amount of money he'd spent on the fan. Tony believed in sacrifice over comfort, and Nick learned of contentment from sacrifice.

"There are people who want to feel the depth of joy and contentment that I feel but don't walk with God in their life," says Nick. "Regardless of their belief systems, I suggest praying and asking God to show you the way toward having that sense of joy. What I know to be true about joy and contentment comes from the Bible. I have tried to fill a void in my life with many different things — people, or adventures such as skydiving and surfing — but what will ultimately fill that void is best told in scripture. In Philippians 4:12-13 of the New Living Translation, Paul, who was innocently detained in prison at the time, wrote, 'I know how to live on almost nothing or with everything. I have learned the secret of living in every situation, whether it is with a full stomach or empty, with plenty or little. For I can do everything through Christ who gives me strength.' This scripture has inspired me ever since I read it, and I still find it rings true today.

"My only motive," Nick continues, "has been serving people because it's God's will. I've become single-minded in submitting to His authority, and He gives me things to do. It is here that I continue to find joy and contentment. I don't give to those in need to be admired by others. It's the God inside of me that should be commended, not me."

> *"Give your gifts in private, and your Father,*
> *who sees everything, will reward you."*
> —Matthew 6:4 NLT

CEOs Concur

When Rick Frishman wrote *Networking Magic,* he interviewed more than 100 CEOs to ask them what message they wanted to express in his book about tapping into the power of personal and professional networks. They all shared a common response. They wanted to teach people about giving without any expected return. In the next chapter, we'll explore business opportunities to give and to help grow organizations and produce profits that benefit all people involved and far beyond.

CHAPTER 6

The Business of Giving

*I*n 1982, Rick Frishman, president of the oldest and largest book publicity firm in the US today, had a partner and mentor who asked him to hire his best friend's son for part-time work, so Rick did. The son's name was Mitch, and he had just graduated from college but was having difficulty finding a job. Rick took him in and taught him how to write press kits and taught him about the book publicity business in general.

"One of the messages we always teach authors is not to bring a book to market for financial gain," Rick says, "but instead do it because you have greater grounds. You want to teach or to help people in some way."

Within about six months' time, Mitch left the company and, not too long afterward, wrote a book of his own. The sole purpose of his book was to give back. Mitch wrote his book to help a friend, Professor Morrie Schwartz, who was diagnosed with Lou Gehrig's disease. Mitch lived in Boston and visited Morrie regularly every Tuesday in Chicago. The purpose of the book was to pay Morrie's medical bills. After paying it forward, he received it back a thousand times over. Eventually Mitch Albom sold more than five million copies of his book, *Tuesdays With Morrie*.

Since then, Mitch has written other books, selling millions of copies and giving millions to the charitable foundations that he started. All of this is a result of his desire to give by helping a friend who was dying of a disease and wanting to pay for his medical expenses.

"Mitch was helped when he didn't have a job," Rick says, "and he paid it forward. Look at him now."

Why Aren't We Rich Yet?

The days of entitlement are over. Just because we exist on this planet doesn't make us worthy of receiving anything from anyone until we make giving a priority and work toward the greater good.

 What are you prepared to give in order to be rich?

The economic times of the twenty-first century started off strong and then took a major dive. To stay in business, we must create win/win situations for customers and the company, and maintain a profit. We must give customers what they really want—*a feeling of good fortune*. We're all in the relationship-building business, no matter the business we're in. People want to do business with those they know, like, and trust, and when two people really *want* to do business together, they do – regardless of minor details.

There are countless ways to create superior feelings in your customers. This chapter provides you with ideas and examples of exceptional business building, corporate and social responsibility, and strategies by which both small and large businesses have grown rich in giving. You've got nothing to lose, and everything to gain, so get ready, get set, give!

Who Are Your Customers?

Your customers are the people who buy your product or service, of course, as well as those with whom you do business or have a relationship. For example, a bank's customers are the people who hold accounts, mortgages, and loans—and their families—as well as the bank's shareholders, employees, managers, the building owner, insurance companies, marketing agencies, contractors, cleaning staff, and so on. Everyone is a customer; therefore I use the term "customer" to include any people with whom a business has relationships.

What is a business? Business refers to commerce, trade, and a commercial or industrial establishment; however for the larger picture of "give and be rich," the term "business" refers to any team working toward the same goal, such as a non-profit organization or a community. Relationships are key to success in any business, so it makes sense that anyone we relate to would be treated as a customer.

The Lifetime Value of a Client

The lifetime value of a client is worth building a solid relationship. The difference between customers and clients is that clients are long-term. They don't just transact once with a business; they support the business over and over again. What is a client worth to you?

Let's say little old Mrs. Henry purchases her tea at her local grocery store once a month. She doesn't have a large grocery bill, only about $50 each month, but she's a loyal customer and chooses this shop over the others in the area. One day, upon noticing that her tea isn't in stock, she consults a clerk, but he simply tells her that what's on the shelf is all that's available for purchase. Mrs. Henry decides to buy her groceries elsewhere, where she can get everything she needs in one stop. It might not seem like a great loss to a grocery store to lose a customer worth only $50 per month. When you add up the months and years, and the influence that

Mrs. Henry might have over other people, you can see the number adds up to something very significant.

$50 x 12 months x 10 years x 10 other people = A $60,000 loss, all over a box of tea.

What if you factor in that there could be other customers like Mrs. Henry who went elsewhere to shop because the service or selection was better? How could this grocery store build a solid foundation for lifetime customers? Let's rethink the scenario.

Mrs. Henry asks a clerk whether her favorite tea is in stock. The clerk gives her full attention to discover what she wants and needs and how the store can accommodate her. The clerk responds that the stock is arriving in a day or so and that the store will deliver a box to her door. They follow through with their promise, and Mrs. Henry pays for the tea and maintains her loyalty to the shop. She also speaks to her social circle about the extra-special service she received, which creates a positive impression in the minds of others about the grocery store. Mrs. Henry feels important, and the staff feel empowered to be able to delight her.

The cost of this is minimal—other than a delivery person's time and fuel—but compared to the high cost of losing a customer, it's a drop in the bucket. The benefits, however, are priceless. The difference between ordinary and extraordinary is that little extra.

What would empowered staff and delighted customers be worth to your business?
What personal services can you offer your customers to create lifetime clients?

"When two people want to do business together, the details don't stand in the way."
—Ken Blanchard

For a business team to be empowered to make these types of decisions (delivering tea to an elderly customer, for example), they must be in sync with the company's overall mission. When all people involved in a business have a laser-sharp focus on their mission, they think within that frame of reference when making decisions. Of course there are policies for safety and budgets and whatnot to consider, but remembering why we got into business in the first place helps raise employee awareness so they think about the larger picture, take ownership, and behave in alignment with the company's overall goals. This may mean raising the roof on your current methodology in business. We must think differently to stay competitive and maintain our market share.

Raising the Roof

Jose and his wife purchased a hot dog cart in hopes of venturing into business. Soon after their first child was born, they decided to use the cart as a vehicle to feed the homeless. At an outreach event for the Salvation Army, Jose got to know Eric, the board chair and a fellow member of his church.

Eric called Jose a couple of weeks later. Jose is a roofing consultant, and Eric needed his help. Eric sat on the board for the Central Florida Urban League, and they were in dire need of a solution to fix a leaky roof that flooded two rooms with every rainstorm that passed over the Orlando area. Jose went to give an objective opinion about the situation, and two things were confirmed; the CFUL building needed a new roof, but they didn't even have a budget to repair the old one.

Jose had a thought. For the past three years, he had worked with a Canadian company, Tri-Thermal Roofing Systems, whose goal was to move their proprietary roofing system into the US marketplace. "Perhaps this could work out as a win/win for both organizations," he told Eric, "and knowing Stan Cox, the Chief Financial Officer of TTR™, he just may be able to help us out."

"Stan, the Central Florida Urban League needs a new roof, and they are interested in your TTR™ system," Jose told Stan.

"Great to hear, Jose. We're interested in that marketplace," replied Stan. "What's their budget?"

"Well, that's a bit of a story. This prospect doesn't have a budget. They're a minority non-profit organization, and they're doing benevolent work in their community, but their assets are in jeopardy with their leaking roof. Although they need a new roof, they can't even afford to repair the one they have. I was wondering if there was something you could do to help."

Local quotes for repair and replacement ranged between $30,000 and $60,000. The Central Florida Urban League provides economic support and education to minorities. Their roof leaked and flooded two rooms each time it rained. That was all Stan Cox knew. "Are these good people?" he asked.

"Eric is an acquaintance from church," Jose explained, "and a generous provider of service to two organizations that serve the under privileged in Orange County. I believe he and his associates are doing God's work."

"Then we'll help them on their mission," declared Stan.

Within weeks, Stan ventured from Ontario to Orlando to meet Allie Braswell, the CEO of the Central Florida Urban League. Stan was impressed to learn of the center's mission and vision. He conversed with Allie on a personal level and, after only thirty minutes, made a commitment. "We'll do your roof for free," he said.

Allie gave thanks with a handshake and shared the news with his organization. "This angel out of the north has answered our prayers," he told them.

The project began six weeks later. One full crew of installers from the Ontario-based, family-operated business Cox Roofing Systems had three generations of roofers working on the CFUL roof. Their mission was to give the CFUL a brand new Tri-Thermal Roofing system, from start to finish, in one week. It was an extreme roofing makeover that would protect the shelter for many years.

"I was filled with a sense of joy to see the partnership forming between the Urban League and Stan Cox," Jose says. "The league officials were humbled to be the recipient of Stan's generosity. They knew that he did not have to give this gift. He could have chosen another customer to apply his patented roofing system. I knew that this was a perfect storm—a confluence of great need by the CFUL, meeting with ideal opportunity for TTR™, grounded in faith, and orchestrated through divine intervention."

The opportunity for TTR™ to raise the roof in a market in which it was interested to showcase its proprietary technology turned into a whole lot more. The leaders of the Urban League felt it incumbent upon them to repay Stan Cox with exposure. So they went knocking on doors, calling friends and associates, and inviting people to come and witness the philanthropic deed as it took place. The mayoral staff, the director of facility of Florida Hospital, various contractors, building owners, economic development partners, and many others were contacted to visit.

Local new agencies gathered to report on the event. "Canadian Company Expanding Into Florida," "Canadian Company Reaches Out to Help Minority Non-profit"—these headlines appeared in newspapers, and the stories started telling themselves. One reporter paid special attention to the spirit of partnership he'd felt by covering the story.

Within one week, the extreme roofing makeover was completed, but the giving was just beginning. In raising the roof with the spirit of generosity and Christian values, this new roof protects state-of-the-art computer equipment in a classroom that will continue to help kids get their high school diploma. It safeguards a room where families are counseled to be able to stay in their homes during an incredible foreclosure crisis in Florida. The new roof has helped maintain jobs for the people who work there; it returns an excellent energy savings; and it adds to the value to the building. It will continue to serve many people for generations.

Since the roofing project has been completed, CEO Allie Braswell informed Jose that the spirit of giving became contagious in their local community. The CFUL playground—what used to be a dirty field—is now home to a beautiful new play system donated by a local company and installed by a team of more than 250 volunteers.

"I never realized that when I partnered these two organizations the result would be so abundant," Jose says "I am personally blessed with the support of a new team of TTR™ supporters, who assist me in my consulting projects. There are so many people who now believe that this is the best roofing system under the sun. We attracted many prospects and even a new sales force for our TTR™ system."

One day Jose overheard John, the sales manager for TTR™, asking Eric, a successful commercial real estate player, "Why do you want to spend your time to help us grow our TTR™ market here in Florida?"

Eric replied, "Because it's something I can believe in."

"I feel rich in the friendships that we have formed. This is the most amazing part in the arrangement for all of us," says Jose. "Our new friend Eric Jackson says, 'The riches that matter most are gracious people—the friendships we've made, meeting fellow Christians, praying before sharing lunch together, thanking God for the people that came together, the food and the opportunity to help our fellow man to make this community a better place. When you do the right things, blessings come back to you.' Little did I know that using our hot dog cart service and meeting Eric would lead to the partnership of raising a roof in so many ways."

How can you raise the roof on your business or service? Is there someone in need whom you can serve by doing what you do best?

Hopefully you can raise the roof in your own community, remembering Stan Cox and his decision to do what he felt was right for his heart rather than for his bank account.

Be and Do, then Have

There is a very popular principle that helps people attain success. It's called "Be, Do, Have." Many people use the opposite strategy—"Have, Do, Be"—in their thought process regarding achieving success. Using this opposite process, Stan Cox would have thought, "If I could *have* a customer in the United States who wanted a roof, then we could *do* our patented roofing system for that customer, and as a result *be* well known for our patented system."

The trouble with this approach is that we cannot always have—or easily have—certain conditions, in order to *do* and *be* what we intend. *Being* means giving first.

In Jose and Stan's story, the company used the Be, Do, Have strategy in a way that brought them tremendous public awareness and exposure. They intended to be well recognized in the US as a provider of a cost-effective, environmentally friendly roofing alternative, and they succeeded by first *being* a supplier of their system, *doing* the installation, and as a result *having* more exposure and opportunities than they'd ever thought possible.

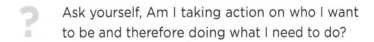 Ask yourself, Am I taking action on who I want to be and therefore doing what I need to do?

If the answer is yes, you'll give and grow rich with what you intend to have as a result.

Define and Design Your Future

In any business, large or small, first define who you want to be, and then walk as if you already are that person and organization. When we are clear in our minds about who we are, where we are going, and how we intend to get there, we tend to get there a lot quicker.

At a youth business seminar I was leading, we held a party one afternoon that was themed "Come as you will be in 2013," which was five years into the future. We encouraged students to dress, talk, and bring props as if they were already living the business goals and dreams they had set up in their business plans. The excitement and fun we had really helped the students feel as if their designs had manifested.

Getting clear about what we're expecting to be, do and have in our future is another way of tapping the circle of abundance. In preparation we determine what we need to give, and by acting out the reality of having it already we feel the excitement as though we've already received. This mental activity jumpstarts the achievement process, and buys us one of the most valuable assets – time!

Buy Back Your Time

If you ask the wealthiest people what one thing they wish they could buy at the end of their lives, most of them probably will answer, "Time." If you ask people at the end of their lives what they would do with more time, most would say they would invest it in the relationships they have with those whom they love. A brilliant secret of the rich is that they figure out the value of their time and then buy it back wholesale.

When you calculate your hourly rate of pay, you will discover opportunities to buy back your time. For example, Troy is self-employed and earns $80,000 per year for forty-eight weeks of work at thirty-five hours per week. His time is worth approximately $47 per hour. How many of those hours don't produce income? What if Troy hired someone at half that amount to buy back other time so he could focus on more work that will produce income? $47 per hour divided in half is $23.50. Troy would essentially buy back an hour of his time for $23.50 and generate another $47.

Imagine if you made more money per hour. You most likely will if you focus on what you are best at and let others do what they are experts at. Tasks such as your income tax, bookkeeping, office cleaning, house cleaning, yard maintenance, vehicle maintenance, website maintenance, event planning, and so on can be completed very effectively by skilled people.

By giving tasks to an expert, the odds are that the quality of their results will be better than what you may have been able to produce yourself, especially outside of your area of expertise. Delegating tasks also frees up your time to do what you love to do and are good at, and it even makes you money.

Love What You Do or Don't Do It

A long time ago, I learned how to cook, clean, and do laundry. After about twelve years of practice, I had mastered the skills to keep a clean and tidy home, and by that point I was expecting my first child. I loved my career and loved the idea of being a mom, but I knew there weren't enough hours in a day or week for me to enjoy both with the added domestic duties that came along with a new family. So I decided to delegate my domestic duties, and we hired a full time live-in caregiver. I bought back my time to focus on my career during business hours, and I could enjoy quality time with my family during personal hours. I love what I do, and I can do more of it because I've given someone else the opportunity to serve with her talents. I've given the gift of doing.

 What tasks have you mastered, or not mastered, that you can hire someone else to help you with? Who can you delegate to and invite to grow with the new responsibility?

Delegating—The Gift of Doing

Professionals do my accounting and website work. This frees up my time and allows me to write material for books and articles and create exceptional seminars, workshops, and keynotes. I invest my time doing what I'm adept at, such as research, marketing, and building relationships. I give others the gift of doing what they do best and happily pay them for their expertise and services.

You can leverage your time by hiring, outsourcing, or delegating and attain more wealth doing what you love to do. When you delegate, two or more people are blessed. You receive the gift of more time, and your delegates receive the gift of nurturing and celebrating their natural talents and abilities.

Perhaps you can give your children the gift of doing laundry or cooking. Isn't that a gift? When they move out on their own, they'll use their gifts of experience with these life skills of laundry and cooking.

Your Emotions Are Your Guidance System

The concept of "Love what you do or don't do it" isn't meant to be taken to such an extreme that you must enjoy absolutely everything you do; rather, it's a guidance system. When you find yourself doing something and you don't feel gratified doing it, perhaps it's an indication that you aren't serving others in alignment with your purpose. Your emotions are your guidance system. Give yourself time for silence to listen and feel out what feels right and what doesn't.

> *"The best cure for too much to do is silence and solitude."*
> **—Unknown**

Let the Experts Help

Giving an open mind to a professional coach certainly has a high return rate. Over the years, I've hired numerous coaches to help me get where I'm going more quickly. For example, as I wrote this book, I worked with a fitness coach, a professional speaking coach, a book writing and marketing coach, and a personal and spiritual life coach. As a result, I have excellent health, a killer keynote speech, and a superb book. I wouldn't have high-quality results trying to do all of this on my own.

Give experts a chance to help you gain the success you're chasing. You'll get where you're intending to go much quicker and with less wasted time and costly mistakes along the way. Life is too short to make mistakes by doing everything yourself. Tap into the wisdom of others who have been there and done that.

Get Hooked on Giving in Business

Crystal, a young entrepreneur I coached for two years, became hooked on giving. Being a pedorthist and running a BioPed clinic gave her the opportunity to help people alleviate painful or debilitating conditions with custom orthotics, orthopedic footwear, and foot care.

The day Crystal met Janice was a life-changing opportunity for both women. Janice was a severe diabetic patient with neuropathy, a loss of sensation in the feet, and was at risk of foot amputation. After trying on specialty footwear, Janice was delighted with new comfort of one pair, yet her mind seemed to be working overtime to find a way to pay for the shoes. Her family had been through a difficult time, but if she saved for six months, she could return and purchase the shoes.

Crystal took a leap toward honorable business practice. "Janice, I want you to walk a mile in my shoes. In fact, I would like you to just take them, walk out of the store with them on, and continue to walk many miles toward better health and comfort."

Janice argued that she couldn't accept the offer of not paying for the shoes, but Crystal convinced her that this is what she does. "I help people live pain-free, and I prevent debilitating problems," she explained. "I have a store full of shoes for people and a closet full of shoes at home for myself. You need these shoes to maintain your feet and prevent amputation."

With tears of joy, Janice left the assessment room and went to tell her husband in the reception area that Crystal had given her the shoes at no charge.

"This was a stellar day for me, and I set a goal to do it once a month to help people with my profession, whether they can afford the treatment or not," Crystal says. "The combination of the gratitude for all I have in my life, including a successful business, a healthy family, shoes galore, and the ability to give some of that to someone in need, grounded me in a sense of happiness that money cannot buy."

Days like these are a constant reminder that Crystal is on the right path and doing the work she was intended to do and serving people to the best of her ability, even if it means putting her best foot forward and putting money aside.

Janice still visits the clinic regularly and has told many of her friends about living with comfort and taking continuous steps toward improving her health. "When she visits, she always dances in her shoes," Crystal says. "When I see her in public, she always tells me how I touched her life with the gift of specialty footwear."

Every step you take on your feet can be a subtle reminder of how blessed you are to have mobility. Can you help someone else have better mobility? Whatever your profession, product, or service, someone out there is in need. Perhaps you can help them walk a mile in your shoes.

Put the Shoes on the Other Feet

You may have heard of the One for One Movement created by Blake Mycoskie, founder of TOMS, Shoes for a Better Tomorrow. In 2006, Blake decided to help children in Argentina by giving them shoes to protect their feet. He started TOMS, a company that vowed to match every pair of shoes sold with a pair of new shoes given to a child in need—one for one. Later that year, Blake traveled to Argentina with family, friends, staff, and 10,000 pairs of shoes. All of this was made possible by TOMS customers.

In developing countries, many children grow up barefoot. Whether they're playing, doing chores, or going to school, these children are at risk of contracting diseases that penetrate skin, cuts, and wounds, all of which can become infected and lead to long-term impairment. Shoes also have value beyond being critical for physical health. Many schools in developing countries require shoes for attendance. Healthy, educated children have a better chance of improving the future of their entire community.

As of September 2010, TOMS customers had given away more than one million pairs of new shoes to children in need. "We are incredibly proud, as well as humbled. So many lives have been changed along the way, and we are inspired each day by the stories," Blake states in the company's 2011 giving report.

This business success story is a profound example of the principle of giving and becoming rich. There are countless riches in the stories of the lives that have been changed because of the people who have bought TOMS shoes

A corporate focus from profitability to social responsibility is like rocket fuel toward a better future.

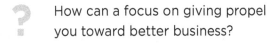

How can a focus on giving propel you toward better business?

"Giving is what fuels us. Giving is our future."
—**Blake Mycoskie**, TOMS Shoes

Strategies for Good

When employees feel their work makes a difference, they're happier doing it. Also, when what they're doing resonates well with their values, they remain motivated and engaged. Corporate giving and social responsibility enhance employee satisfaction and productivity and increase motivation and commitment, writes Susan Hyatt in her book *Strategy for Good: Business Giving Strategies for the 21st Century.*

Employees are just as concerned as consumers about the behavior of their company. Getting involved in community giving engages workers and has a significant positive impact on improved communications, teambuilding, relations between management and employees, company reputation, recruitment, and retention. Corporate social responsibility is also a stress reliever in the workplace.

Smiles For Life

The Callander Bay Dental Centre, located on the shore of Lake Nipissing, Ontario, has been enriched through giving thousands of dollars each year to children's charities, both locally and internationally. This has brought the clinic an abundance of success, immeasurable team morale and spirit, community exposure, and leadership—not to mention a donation of $44,500 to a worthy cause, a one-year record.

In 1999, the dental clinic became involved with Smiles For Life. Through this charitable program, dental professionals whiten teeth to raise money for children who are seriously ill, disabled, or underprivileged in their communities and around the world.

"It's a lot of work, but the team chooses to take it on year after year because they are moved by the feeling of making such a difference with their skills and abilities," says manager Suzanne Harmony. "Two team members sacrifice their lunch hour everyday from March to June each year. They rotate their days, so the whole team gets involved in donating their time, energy, and effort."

For example, a hygienist might team up with an assistant on their scheduled day. They take impressions on patients, pour the molds, then stay late to trim models and make the custom-fit whitening trays so that every customer has a personal kit to whiten their teeth. All proceeds are given directly to the charities associated with Smiles For Life.

Between March and June of each year, hundreds of dental practices professionally whiten teeth and raise money for underprivileged children. They're members of the Crown Council, an alliance of leading-edge dental teams that passionately serve through charitable work. Fifty percent of the charitable donations raised can serve right in the community where the dental office practices, and the other half goes to international programs, shared among recipients across the country such as the Hospital for Sick Kids and the Camp Trillium fund.

The channels of giving are endless with this program, Suzanne says. "For example, we have a regular donor who doesn't qualify for our whitening program because he has crown and bridge work, yet he still donates $250 to the program and allows us to determine who would be a recipient of the whitening. This year, the team cried knowing they were doing the right thing as they chose a gentleman in our community who had a cervical spine injury. His life slid downward after the injury, and the opportunity to whiten his smile gave him a huge boost in self-esteem.

Philanthropy drives team morale. It provides one common goal to work together toward, beyond our mission of the dental practice, and our team is constantly pulled together in the spirit of generosity."

The Leader in You

No matter your position, you have the privilege of giving influence. When you learn to influence other people in a positive way, you begin to lead. Leadership is both a concept and a way of action; it's what you do that makes you a distinguished leader. People have asked me whether leaders are born or developed, and my response is that leadership is the result of a choice we all make. It is possible that some people have more natural leadership skills and attributes than others.

Communication combined with leadership skills are the multiplier of performance. Leadership is influence—nothing more, nothing less. You, and everyone in your company, have a certain degree of influence, and you don't need to be in a position of authority to exercise it.

Tina and Tommy work for an organization as gatekeepers, answering incoming calls and attending to walk-in traffic. Do they have the ability to lead the organization? The answer is yes; Tina and Tommy influence all incoming calls and customer perceptions, as well as internal relations with their colleagues and managers. They are leaders, or at least they certainly can be leaders when they are taught and develop the skill of influencing others.

While everyone matures into leadership at their own pace, the choices they make toward this maturity can be taught and learned. Everyone has the power to make these choices. Here are a few examples of choices that enhance our ability to influence others:

- authenticity
- integrity
- honesty
- humility
- respect
- consistency
- passion for who you are
- responsibility

When someone chooses to be influential, they take responsibility for a task at hand and do what's necessary to bring that task to completion. If the task fails, the leader also can take responsibility for that and doesn't attempt to place blame on other people or circumstances.

Leadership is where the change happens within a person's life and within an organization's life. When individuals make the choice to change, they feel better about themselves as they recognize their potential to lead their own lives. When individuals feel in control of themselves, they also feel more free to continue to create the life they want to live. I've always said that the only security we have is within ourselves. We must take responsibility.

Having more leaders enhances employees' engagement, productivity, and profitability. Successful businesses quickly make leaders of everyone in their organization. Make the choice today to be more influential. No matter your position in your organization, you can make a difference, and it starts with the leader in you.

Give Enthusiasm

How can I engage my employees?
How can I get my employees to take ownership of their role within
the company?
How can we get people to want to come to work?

These are the questions I get asked often of management. The answer is simple: *give*. Give employees a voice. Ask what would engage them. Ask how they could take better ownership of their roles within the company. Ask what makes them want to come to work.

A research strategy that helps me gather related information before a keynote speech or seminar for a dedicated client is to ask the employees what it would take to increase their department profit by 10 percent. Ten answers that can be implemented from ten departments can translate to a 100 percent increase.

Be enthusiastic. It's contagious.

> *"In the workplace, if you're not fired with*
> *enthusiasm, you'll be fired...with enthusiasm."*
> **—Anonymous** small business owner

Give Your Employees a Voice

Frontline workers often have correct solutions for problem-solving where their roles are concerned. Administrators have answers to their challenges; managers have their answers; and so on throughout the entire company. The two main reasons for giving employees a voice concerning performance, profitability, and change are 1) they already have knowledge, information, and experience; and 2) people believe their own data. When you involve them and ask for their data, they share it and take ownership of the results. In a survey of 200 top companies, a feeling of "being in on things" was rated as the second highest motivator for employee satisfaction.

People ask me these questions all the time:

How can I get my manager to understand my workload?
How can I get ahead in my workplace or career?
How can I manage all the different personalities in the workplace?

Give the best you have to offer to your profession. Take responsibility, stop pointing the blame, give yourself the gift of constant and never-ending improvement, and become the best professional you can be.

Business of the Future

There's a new norm in business, and it starts with giving. I interviewed Andrew Patricio, founder of BizLaunch, Canada's largest small business training company.

Penny: What does "give and be rich" mean to you?

Andrew: You cannot just live and take. You've got to give and take, and the more you give, the better off it will be for you. For example, I gave my time to help universities, speak at conferences, become a CYBF mentor, help at schools, become a social media activist, and deliver webinars—all for free to help people gain valuable insights to building small businesses. This all began with a speech in Toastmasters on the topic of how small business will change the economy, and someone in the audience approached me to speak at the university. I fell in love with the kids and the work and ended up taking over the local business center for seven years.

Penny: Can you think of a role model for this concept of giving first to gain an edge in business?

Andrew: BizLaunch is a super role model. Everything we do is free. We do seminars in stores like Staples, which people attend for free. Now Staples even gives free gift cards to attendees just for coming to learn.

Penny: If everything you give away is free, how do you make money to sustain the business?

Andrew: We get large companies like Staples, VISA, ADP, and Deluxe to pay for the content we produce. It's a fabulous marketing tool for them.

Penny: What is one thing that a business owner can give away to strengthen their business?

Andrew: Give away one or two sessions of your time for free. You have to give in order to get back. This builds trust. When you educate your customer well enough, they can make an informed choice.

Penny: What advice would you give on how to build mutually supportive relationships that work for everyone involved?

Andrew: Give away valuable information to your clients and prospects in exchange for their contact information. Once you have a big enough database, you don't need to find new customers.

I took Andrew's advice in giving a session of my time to invite coaching clients to experience a session before making a commitment to continue, and I even confirmed his last suggestion with my own success story.

Working on Purpose

In 2004, I made a conscious decision to stop working for money and start working on purpose. My desire is to help millions of people develop their unlimited potential, so I decided to write an article about time management and share it with as many people as I could. I called up my friend Paul Barton, a disciplined columnist for our community paper. Over lunch, I shared my article with him.

"I want to encourage you to keep writing regularly," he said. "By consistently creating written material, you will soon have an inventory, and that will be something you can leverage."

At that moment, I made a commitment to continue with a monthly article, with the purpose of fulfilling my mission. My articles give away my information for free and educate people on my philosophy of "give and be rich" and my corporate program, Workplace Relationships: Strategies for Improving Communication and Customer Relations.

This has been the most powerful advertising and referral system that drives revenue for my companies. I have proven that when you use your talents to serve humanity, permanent abundance follows. This was my unique way of working on purpose and not for money.

The result? My income doubled within the first year and continues to grow every year because of the readership of many thousands of subscribers who enjoy my gift each month. I've positioned myself as an expert in my field of workplace relationships, and I've built an inventory of hundreds of articles. My material is circulated electronically, and my articles are published regularly in newspapers, magazines, and global trade journals. All of this is a result of giving my information away for free consistently and with no expected return.

 What can you give away or share to build your business?

Are you active in social media for your business? Do you offer people value in your conversations, tweets, blogs, or Facebook posts? Or do you just advertise? Knowledge is easier than ever to share with people, either face-to-face or using technology. Think first about what you can give to someone that will add value to their life for the time they invest in reading, watching, or listening to your message for a few short minutes.

How Do I Become Rich?

When you read biographies of people who have created amazing success in their lives, such as Mother Teresa, Anthony Robbins, Steve Jobs, and Bill Gates, it's motivating to know that they are human, just like you, and that you have the same possibility and potential. They found a need, filled it, and had passion, persistence, and determination. We can all do that. The part that many people have a difficult time getting over is "How do I get rich doing it?"

One day I had an epiphany. Mother Teresa, one of my all-time favorite role models, wasn't wealthy. She was world-renowned for her giving and making an enormous difference in the world and was happy with minimal possessions. All the money given to her was promptly given to those in need.

> *"If you can't feed a hundred people, then feed just one."*
> —**Mother Teresa**

Do You Feel Stuck?

By overcoming the hurdle of not needing to have money to be successful and not needing to know in advance how my service to others would repay me millions of dollars, I could move forward in doing what I needed to do—serve others with my unique talents.

I was on course, able to believe that the universe has a perfect accounting system and that I would be justly rewarded for my efforts that I'd spent doing beneficial work. Whether or not I earned millions, I could still satisfy my desire for helping millions of people develop their unlimited potential, and in believing in this, I let go of my attachment to money.

If you feel stuck in the "How will I get rich?" mentality, change your thoughts to

> How can I give more of myself to serve others?
> How can I use my talents to serve humanity?
> Where do I need to value myself more, to feel more valuable?
> How can I help?

Don't think about the money. The money will come. The universe has a perfect accounting system in which no good deed goes unmatched. This is law. Release your attachment to needing to have money. Feeling rich in giving is possible for anyone. With that feeling, wealth can be created. Riches take all types of shapes and qualities in one's life: money, relationships, health, vitality, opportunities, and much more. The riches will come; you have my promise.

Regardless of the type of business you choose to make your living, your intention to give to others is key. If you do the right thing day after day, the money will come.

The Human Side of Your Customer

We've been so caught up in the chase for profit that we often forget why we got into business in the first place. Hopefully we entered into business as an entrepreneur or an interested employee, because we wanted to help solve a problem for our customer. Yet many companies have lost track of the customer and instead focus more of their attention on the bottom line. This is not a win/win situation. It's win/lose. You win and the customer loses. How long do you expect that model to work?

How Do We Touch the Human Side of a Customer?

In his bestselling book *Megatrends*, John Naisbett predicted that successful businesses of the future needed to be both "high tech and high touch."

Touch the human side of your customer to let them know you care about them as a person or that you thought of them, and not with another sale flyer or promotion notice. Just build the relationship. People are creatures of emotion, fueled by pride and vanity. When we feed their emotions, they feel good. You've heard that people won't necessarily remember what you've told them or done for them, but they will always remember how you made them feel—whether it's good or bad.

Touching someone's emotional side means recognizing them as a person first and a business associate second. Increase your client retention and referrals by acknowledging and appreciating the human side of your consumers.

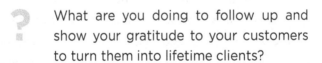

What are you doing to follow up and show your gratitude to your customers to turn them into lifetime clients?

Eight Reasons to Thank Your Customers

Thanking people satisfies one of the top needs of the human spirit—the need to be appreciated, understood, and cared about. When people feel this need has been met, they reciprocate.

When I reach out and connect with people and acknowledge, appreciate, and honor them, they feel valued and they remember me.

Therefore, they refer me to others because they know and like me and I've gained a sense of their trust. By my having given them a positive emotional experience, they remember me. Thanking your customers is one of those opportunities in which showing appreciation (saying thank you) wins over self-promotion (advertising).

There are many reasons to thank your customers. Here are eight of them.

1. Each time a customer does business with you, send a thank-you greeting card or postcard to let them know you appreciate their business, or, as I say in mine, "Thank you for your trust in us."
2. When a customer refers business to you, thank them every time. Customers who refer you should feel very special. Word of mouth is free and gives you instant credibility.
3. Thank your customer when they appreciate you, your business, or service by paying you a compliment. Often people are reluctant to accept a compliment, but the best response to a compliment is "Thank you."
4. When a customer makes you smile, tells you a joke, or gives you some form of inspiration, thank them.
5. Suggestions or new recommendations from a customer's point of view are very valuable feedback. Thank people who step out of their comfort zone to let you know how things can be improved. Rather than being insulted, be delighted that they shared their opinion with you. You might say, "I appreciate your feedback about our product or service and want to thank you for taking the time to share your opinion. Our priority is customer satisfaction, and comments like those you provided help us become better at our business. We sincerely appreciate your bringing this to our attention."

6. If your recommendation is acted upon by a customer, thank them for their trust in you. A follow-up card is an efficient way to let them know you care and are open to hearing more from them.

7. When customers say "no" to you, thank them. Keep the door wide open for them to return for business by sending them a card of thanks. For example, you might say or write, "Thank you for thinking of me to request a quote for services. I respect your decision to support a competitor. If I can be of any assistance to you in the future, please do not hesitate to contact me. Your success is important." What have you got to lose? You've already lost the deal, so let them know they can feel comfortable to approach you in the future.

8. When a customer issues a complaint or shows impatience toward your product or service, thank them. They're giving you a nudge toward better business and better service. Take their feedback very seriously, and examine whether it's worth acting on. Feedback is one person's opinion. If a customer is very unsatisfied to the point of sharing the reason with you, you can celebrate, because they could have left your business without comment, and you never would have known why. You might send a card that apologizes for the mix-up or oversight, or one that thanks the customer for their feedback and lets them know the company is considering a resolution for the future. If they're the type of customer you're sure you can afford to lose for a lifetime, thank them with a card that provides your competitors' contact information.

These tips are definitely "high touch." Thanking people satisfies their need to be appreciated. You will have given them a sense of pride, and they'll always remember how you made them feel.

Strike an Emotional Chord with a Card

When was the last time a company that values your business sent you an unexpected personalized greeting card, note, or gift? Less than 3 percent of mail that comes into a household is personalized; the rest is unsolicited junk mail and bills or statements. When was the last time you received a phone call from a business or friend just to say "I was thinking about you"? In the busy world of business, few people seem to find time for the personal touch, but those who do are more effective—more influential, more liked, more referred, and paid more money.

Send your customers cards, handwritten notes, business thank-you cards, or gifts, or pick up the phone and call them. It's a marketing strategy that's sure to strike an emotional chord, and it will have lasting results. People do business with those whom they know, like, and trust. The best way to get someone to know, like, and trust you is to help them feel good about themselves. Appreciate people. It's a gift that's free or costs very little—and one that's useful, saved, and cherished forever.

It's Raining Referrals

Do you have a referral system? Most businesses don't have a formal system for thanking the clients who trust them enough to refer them to their friends. Treat your referral sources in a very special way. Send a personal card to appreciate their trust in you, or send a gift or discount—whatever you decide. Create a system and implement it for a full year. Then evaluate its success and change it up slightly to suit your needs and offer something different, year after year, for those who continue to send you prospects.

Find a way to stand out from other businesses, and make people feel very special for referring you to their friends. I often see this sign in businesses: "The greatest compliment our customers can give us is a referral."

The Sales Pitch Turned Inside Out

Traditional business-building thinking equates to advertising: "Let's get out there and promote the business, talk to people, tell them who we are, what we do, and how they'll benefit."

But times are changing. In my own advertising campaigns, I've tried a new strategy, and it works. My strategy is simply to appreciate and give to people, and it's much more powerful than traditional advertising. In fact, it returns more revenue, product sales, referrals, and opportunities than I'd ever manifested in the past.

At a local group luncheon, I had ten minutes to present my business. I decided to turn my sales pitch inside out and make the presentation about the group. "In recognition of all the members who have supported and helped me, and for my clients in the room, I am grateful for your contributions to my success," I told them. "I would like to thank this club for its many referrals and support of my programs."

The result? I didn't have to promote myself, my service, or my products like an infomercial. I accomplished this indirectly by recognizing others, sold lots of products, and continue to receive respect and referrals from this group. As a bonus, I felt fantastic about having verbally appreciated everyone.

 How can you turn your sales pitch inside out and make it about giving to others, rather than having them give to you?

Is Your Net Working?

"Networking" can be defined as the development of relationships or the exchange of information to further a career. Many people think they are networking by exchanging business cards, but doing this is only one in a series of necessary steps to be effective with your networking effort.

Through the years I have learned that people buy what they are familiar with and buy from those they know, like, and trust. After exchanging business cards, at least four important steps are required to further a career, make a sale, or transform a contact into a customer. Let's break them down.

First, have a plan. Who do you want to meet? Where do they network? Who do you know who knows them? What is their business? Give time and effort to research and plan your networking strategy.

Second, spend face-to-face time with your contact (we'll call them a prospect for now). Talk about their favorite subject (themselves). For the purpose of networking, specifically find out about their business. Listen carefully. I can't emphasize this enough—really listen. If you miss something, ask them to tell you again. They'll have no problem repeating themselves, because you're talking about their favorite subject—themselves. After listening until they've finished speaking, restate what you've heard them tell you. This proves that you're listening and that you seek to really understand their business.

"The greatest need of the human spirit is the need to feel understood," writes Stephen R. Covey in his acclaimed book *The 7 Habits of Highly Effective People*. "Seek first to understand, then to be understood" is the fourth habit, but when it comes to interdependence (i.e., mutual dependence or our ability to coexist effectively and productively with others), consider it the most important. Give people a feeling that you care enough to invest your attention and interest in them.

Third, after meeting a prospect, follow up. You've probably heard the phrase "The third time's the charm." In advertising and marketing, this means that someone must hear about your product or service three times before they feel familiar with it.

After you've taken the time to learn something about your prospect's business, the fourth and final step is to make contact with the intention of letting them know you're interested or care about them. In this age of technology, we have many mediums with which to do this: via Twitter, Facebook, Google Plus, text messages, email, fax, telephone, snail mail, or in person. There are so many choices, so how do you choose? Electronic media is quick and cost-effective, but it's also overused and less personal. When was the last time someone took the time to send you a handwritten note? How much more attention and importance do people give a handwritten, snail-mailed note over an email or text message?

If you want to make a lasting impression, consider some old-fashioned social grace like Sharon did as she built a relationship with cartoonist Lynn Johnston. Send a card or a note in appreciation for meeting your new prospect, or pick up the phone and make person-to-person contact to let your prospect know you're thinking about them.

The online greeting card system I use creates a real greeting card in minutes, for less than a dollar, that is personalized with my message, handwriting, and signature. I can even add photos of people to create keepsakes that will last a lifetime for the recipient. An actual card arrives by snail mail in my prospect's mailbox within a week of my having met them and sending the card. I don't ask for their business yet. I just share my appreciation for having met them, acknowledge their effort in business, or somehow celebrate them as a person or business.

Stay in touch with your customers and business contacts. Find reasons to stay in touch with people you want to have in your business relationship circle by focusing on what you can give them. For example, you care about the success of their business, don't you? You could call someone days after meeting them and say something along the lines of, "Hi, Ted. This is Penny Tremblay from the Tremblay Leadership Center. We met at the Chamber of Commerce after-hours event yesterday, and after hearing more about your upcoming annual meeting this summer, I wanted to share an article I read in the Northern Ontario Business publication. Can I send it to you?"

You could also offer to deliver the article if you'd like to meet with the person face-to-face.

Referrals are a first-choice gift to give a business contact, so you could also tell your prospect, "I've developed quite an extensive database, and I'm constantly trying to connect one client with another. How would I recognize the perfect client for you?"

Like the Energizer bunny who keeps going and going and going, a good business relationship strategy is to keep giving, and giving and giving.

Ask for What You Want

By now you've invested time in attending a networking event, listened, and sought to understand your prospect's business. You've also made time to follow up to let your prospect know you're interested in—and, more importantly, care about—their business. You're earning the privilege of a face-to-face meeting with your prospect. Take the opportunity.

Many people are fearful of making a phone call to ask for business or to sell something—most likely because they haven't given anything first, so they feel they're only taking. Are you fearful to give a gift? Probably not. If you're rooted in giving and have a genuine concern for someone else's business and success, you won't feel reluctance but rather an eagerness to help.

Follow up After the Sale

Hopefully you've converted your prospect to a long-term client based on the relationship you've established and continue to invest in. Whether or not this is the case, record this contact into your contact manager. Include all the information you have about the contact so far, such as phone and fax numbers, mailing addresses, where you met the person, and what you remember about your conversation.

Your prospect or client will be impressed in two or three months time when you make contact again and remember something about your last conversation. You could say something such as, "Hi. The last time we spoke you were preparing for your annual meeting. How did that work out for you?"

When people feel appreciated, understood, and cared about, they reciprocate. When you reach out and connect with people—acknowledge them, appreciate them, and honor their progress—they feel good about themselves and remember you. Therefore, they have the familiarity to refer you to others because they know and like you, and you'll already have gained their trust. Don't just exchange business cards; take the steps necessary to convert business cards into long-term clients by building relationships.

First in Mind, First in Choice

The number-one reason customers lose loyalty to your business is that they feel you took their business for granted. The number-two reason is that they forgot about you.

What are you doing to stay first in mind, first in choice with your customers that's different from the marketing whirlwind of ads, mailings, email campaigns, and social networking and media outreach?

Go for Win/Win

Let's keep it simple. In any relationship, personal or business, both parties must grow or gain in some way. This is win/win. When people grow interdependently, they become valuable members of a family, community, or workplace because they can work together, communicate effectively, and find mutually beneficial solutions to problems and challenges.

We have learned to believe the fallacy that there is only so much pie to go around, and that a bigger piece for me is best. If that's the case, that means someone else loses. What if we learned that we can all eat the pie and enjoy it together? It's a lot more fun that way and doesn't leave a bad aftertaste in our mouths. I challenge you to go for a win/win resolution in any conflict situation.

By listening to and understanding another human being, you accept and praise them for their position in the circumstance, and that alone is a powerful start to finding a solution that works in the highest and best interest of everyone and everything involved.

Every negotiation should have a win/win outcome in order to create the best relationships; all parties involved must grow. You have a critical responsibility to take a win/win mentality into all business arrangements if the survival of your business is in your forecast for the next ten to twenty years. Those who grasp on to that mentality will have infinite success. The days of harsh negotiation, in which one person wins at the expense of another, are long gone.

Win/Win Requires Both Giving and Receiving

Giving in business is key to sustainable growth. Your gifts, given to others, create and circulate abundant wealth. There are two dynamics in exchanging energies and currencies. Giving is first, and receiving is next. You can't have one without the other.

In order for a business arrangement to be a win for you, you must be willing to receive your part. This is more difficult than giving for some people. Being addicted to giving is a dangerous recipe for business. For example, some people in business have a difficult time valuing themselves. They price their service too low, or give too much for too little, and because the balance of giving and receiving is off, their business balance sheet is also off.

Receiving is an answer to that which we ask for. It is exactly in proportion to the value we place on ourselves, and it is abundantly provided when we have a purpose for the riches, especially when a portion is re-gifted back into the circle of abundance.

For business or life in general, make time to contemplate this important question:

 How much are you willing to receive and why?

Go, Give, and Be Rich

I hope this book has inspired you to believe that no matter who or where you are in your life, you already have the ability to give and receive more. You may only need to remember, to feel, and to see the experiences of others who have become rich by giving, or to create an open and inviting space that will allow you to receive more.

Through giving, you'll feel worthy and deserving to receive the best that life offers. You must receive to complete the circulation of abundance. If you don't receive, you'll block the flow. Accept what comes into your life, and be grateful for it. It may not seem like a gift at first, because it may require you to make a change, such as accepting an illness, an uncomfortable experience, or constructive feedback. On the other hand, the gift may be wonderful and easy to accept. In fact anything we are given can be wonderful when we choose to accept it in that way.

By investing in yourself, giving to others and receiving abundantly, we can raise the world's vibration toward love and peace. Go, give, and be rich.

What Is One Thing You Can Give Away and Still Keep?

The answer is your word. Give your word that you will take inspired action to give more, receive more, and become more to circulate abundance starting today.

Share your stories at www.GiveAndBeRich.com. We want to hear from you. What are your "Give and Be Rich" stories? How has this book changed something for you in your life? Let us know.

Contact Information
Penny Tremblay, ACG, CL
Director, Tremblay Leadership Center
180 Shirreff Ave. Suite #230
North Bay, Ontario P1B 7K9 Canada
Email: **penny@pennytremblay.com**
Websites:
   www.PennyTremblay.com
   www.GiveAndBeRich.com

Twitter: ptremblay
Facebook: www.facebook.com/thetremblayleadershipcenter
Google Plus: GiveAndBeRich

MORE ABOUT

Penny Tremblay

Penny lives with her family in North Bay, Ontario. She is Founder and Director of the Tremblay Leadership Center in Ontario, Canada, an international speaker, author, trainer and mentor with more than 20 years experience on the subject of Workplace Relationships. Since 2004 Penny has written and circulated monthly articles electronically to many thousands of subscribers as well as to international trade journals, and ezines. A collection of over 125 articles attract a global audience to her website, www.PennyTremblay.com.

Penny has achieved the highest communication designation available from Toastmasters International, and has been entertaining and educating audiences with speaking engagements and seminars internationally since 1997.

In 2007 Penny co-authored the first, *You're My Hero*™ book in the series, with Barry Spilchuk, author of *A Cup of Chicken Soup for the Soul*. Through the launch of this book and its continued sales, over $27,000 has been donated to charitable organizations to support women and children causes.

Seminars: How would it change your workplace if all of the relations were positive and productive? In seminar or workshop format, participants learn the fundamental elements of building positive rapport and strong relationships with others, resulting in healthy, productive, and profitable relationships.

Mentoring: Relationships are key to success in any business. Refined and polished communicators become leaders and assets to any organization or business. Gain the knowledge and confidence required to build positive rapport and strong workplace relations, one on one with Penny as your guide.

Speaking Engagements: Enjoy an abundance of success and happiness by giving it out first to yourself and others. These motivational and inspiring keynotes relate natural laws and guiding principles to memorable stories and real-life examples.

APPENDIX A

Supporting Activities to Give and Be Rich

Who Am I? (Activity)

Spend some time journaling about who you are as a warm-up for the next activity. When first asked, most people refer to who they are in terms of the roles they play or the accomplishments they've made (e.g., I am a mother of three, a professional speaker...) Furthermore, your body is part of you, but it is not you. If you lost a limb, would you still be you? Look deeper—beyond your roles, your experiences, and your physical body—at who you really are. This kind of close examination requires a connection to your soul, your source energy, your God, or your guidance system. Inhabit that place, where you can think about what makes up your heart and feelings, what drives you to be the best version of yourself. In this place you'll become one with your spirit. Your spirit is who you really are. Your spirit guides you to feel good when you're doing the right things and when you're serving your purpose.

Get to know yourself at the core level. Use the following space to write down who you *really* are. You can include your roles, talents, emotions and feelings, as well as what you love to give to others.

_____

_____

_____

_____

_____

_____

_____

_____

_____

_____

_____

_____

_____

_____

_____

_____

_____

_____

_____

_____

_____

_____

_____

_____

What Do I Want? (Three-Step Activity)

In most of my seminars, we do an exercise called "I Want." During this exercise, people partner up and one person asks the other over and over again, "What do you want?" and then records their answers for them. After several minutes of rhyming off things you want, it gets more difficult. After the material things—such as a new car, a million dollars, or traveling the world—people start to think on a deeper level. *Surely there's more to life than this short list*, they think.

The power in this "I Want" exercise is that you already are all of these things. Your desire came from somewhere, and that somewhere was the depth of your thoughts and feelings. This list of aspirations IS who you really are.

Most people spend more time planning a vacation than they spend planning their entire life. Yet if you give yourself the time necessary, you can plan and design exactly what you want for yourself. You are the creator of your life experience. You are able to choose for yourself.

So what do you want?

The following is a very powerful lesson in personal planning. How will you know what to choose to do with your time, and how to respond (versus react) to circumstances, if you don't have an idea of your desired outcome?

Step 1: What Do I Want to Be, Do, and Have in my Lifetime?

Imagine a genie will grant you any wishes. There are no limits, so go beyond the ones you hold in your mind. Money is not an issue and no one can hold you back. You can be, do, and have anything you can imagine, as long as it's fair and has good intentions.

See the examples of things wanted in the first column of the table below, and then their affirmative version, as if they were already received, with adjectives to describe how it feels to already have them. Make a list in the first column of everything you want. Include what you want to be, do, and have. Write one on each row, use the present tense, and include feeling words to describe what it feels like to have it already.

Step 2: What Will I Give? (What Will I Do?)
To move you closer to what you want to receive in Step 1, write down what you are willing to give, or what action(s) you will take.

Step 3: What Will I Allow Myself to Receive?
(Why Am I Worthy and Deserving?)
To build self esteem around being willing to receive what you want (Step 1) and confidence that you are capable of achieving it (Step 2), write what you are willing to receive and why you are worthy and deserving of having it.

There are two examples to learn from in the following table, and a blank table for your own list, or you can use any paper just by drawing columns.

I Want... (Include your feelings and affirm having already received it.)	I Give... (What Will I Give? What Will I Do?)	I Receive... (What Will I Allow Myself to Receive? Why Am I Worthy and Deserving?)
Example: <u>great health and vitality</u> I feel energized to do the things I want to do with great health and vitality.	I give my awareness to how I'm feeling and act accordingly. When I feel good, I know I'm doing the right things. When I'm not feeling good, I make different choices. I give myself great thoughts, healthy food, nutrition, rest, and respect.	I allow all of the guiding messages and great health and vitality that my body, mind and spirit will provide. I deserve to live with great health and vitality because I have given effort and focus to earn it. With this energy, I will have more to give to others.
Example: <u>new hybrid BMW</u> I feel free in my new blue, hybrid BMW four-door sedan.	I give the best service to my clients, so that I can help them improve their lives and so I can feel good about my contribution to society. I give my old vehicle to someone who needs it and I give rides to some people in need of transportation.	I am worthy of luxury. I love beautiful things, and honor and appreciate seeing other people enjoy their luxury items. Because I give the best service to my clients, I appreciate the best products and services available.

I Want... (Include your feelings and affirm having already received it.)	I Give... (What Will You Give? What Will You Do?)	I Receive... (What Will You Allow Yourself to Receive? Why Are You Worthy and Deserving?)
Continue with your list ...		

APPENDIX B

Activity: Compliment Card Circles

Try this ten-minute activity in your workplace during staff meetings, morning huddles, or training sessions to have fun giving and receiving compliments.

Arrange everyone in a circle. Give each person an index card and have them write their name at the top. Pass the card to the person on your left. Write a compliment for the person whose card you now have. Then pass the card to the left again. Continue to circulate the cards until everyone in the group has had a chance to write a short compliment about the person who owns each card. When the cards are returned to their owners, you'll notice a shift in the energy of the room. People will be excited, talkative, laughing, and smiling.

Ask the people in the room three questions:

1. "How did it feel to give these compliments?" (They'll respond, "Good.")

2. "How did it feel to receive these compliments?" (They'll again respond, "Good.")

3. "If it feels so good to give and receive compliments, why don't we make it a regular part of our day?" (This last question is a rhetorical question intended to get people to think about the huge power in small efforts to recognize and appreciate others.)

Making a Living Through Giving

A Special Report on SendOutCards

My colleague Susan Hyatt is a social impact specialist at the business non-profit CONNECTIONS, Inc. She's always on the lookout for companies that demonstrate profitability and philanthropy. I'm dedicating the next few pages to one such company that I discovered while I was researching this book.

Do you remember Victor Kiam of Remington Shavers? While researching Remington, he was so impressed that he bought the company. I was so impressed with the SendOutCards corporate philosophy and how they show up in the marketplace that I became a distributor myself.

"I'm really frustrated," a new distributor often says to Jordan Adler, the top income earner in the multilevel marketing business SendOutCards.

"Why?" Jordan responds.

"Well, I attended Kody's Treat 'em Right seminar, and I know I'm not supposed to give with the expectation of getting anything in return. I've been giving and giving, but I'm not getting anything back."

"So you're saying you're giving without the intention of getting something back from others, but you're frustrated because you're not getting anything back?" Jordan then tells the new distributor that he is not, in fact, giving to give. "The problem with this approach is that your intention has to be simply to give, period. Don't look for anything in return."

With SendOutCards, when we give, we create a card using an online system; personalize it with a message, photos, and signature; and sometimes even add a gift. When you hit the "send" button, you're not waiting on any level for the phone to ring. You're not expecting a thank-you, credit, feedback, or acknowledgement—it's just a simple gesture of giving.

When you reach out in kindness, the energy of the universe gives back many times over. Often it doesn't come back the way you'd expected; sometimes you look specifically at the individual you gave to, but you may find that being generous in one particular area of your life comes back to you in a completely different area.

Giving and receiving are an exchange of energy. What can you give in your business to help people without having any attachment to getting anything back?

Can I Really Make a Living Through Giving?

You *can* make a living through giving. Recognizing and empowering the human side of people has made a very significant contribution to my career and business, positioned me as a leader in my field, and given me significant monetary rewards.

There are many ways to make a living through giving, including giving in service, sharing your unique talents, giving care to people, or giving effective speeches or training sessions. The options are endless.

How would you like to make a living by sending out cards of acknowledgment and teaching people how to do the same?

You can earn an income with an opportunity from SendOutCards that includes a retail program and a multiplatform leadership incentive. The tools are available for those who want to build a residual income hinged on the values of appreciation and gratitude. The company is on a crusade of changing lives, one card at a time. It just so happens that financial rewards and an abundance of many other riches come along with it.

The SendOutCards system taps into the power of the Internet and technological advancements, and its efficiency does not compromise personal handwriting, signatures, or even personal photos and video. I use it every day.

Touch the human side of your customer to let them know you care about them as a person, or that you thought of them, and not with another sale flyer or promotion notice. Just build the relationship and be rich in all the ways that really matter.

Bibliography

Referenced Books

Beach Money: Creating Your Dream Life Through Network Marketing, Jordan Adler

Billion Dollar Smile: A Complete Guide to Your Extreme Smile Makeover, Dr. Bill Dorfman

Chicken Soup for the Soul books, Jack Canfield and Mark Victor Hansen

Excuse Me, Your Life Is Waiting: The Astonishing Power of Feelings, Lynn Grabhorn

Manifesting for Non-Gurus: How to Quickly & Easily Attract Lasting Results, Robert MacPhee

Megatrends: Ten New Directions Transforming Our Lives, John Naisbett

Networking Magic: Find the Best—From Doctors, Lawyers, and Accountants to Homes, Schools, and Jobs, Rick Frishman

Promptings: Your Inner Guide to Making a Difference, Kody Bateman

Real Moments: Barbara De Angelis

Revelations for a New Millennium: Saintly and Celestial Prophecies of Joy and Renewal, Andrew Ramer

Strategy for Good: Business Giving Strategies for the 21st Century, Susan A. Hyatt

Swim With the Sharks Without Being Eaten Alive: Outsell, Outmanage, Outmotivate, and Outnegotiate Your Competition, Harvey Mackay

The 4-Hour Work Week, Timothy Ferriss

The 5 Levels of Leadership: Proven Steps to Maximize Your Potential, By John C. Maxwell

The 7 Habits of Highly Effective People: Powerful Lessons in Personal Change, Stephen R. Covey

THE cANCER DANCE: What Do You Do When Cancer Catches You With Your Pants Down, Barry Spilchuk

Think and Grow Rich, Napoleon Hill

Tuesdays With Morrie, Mitch Albom

You're My Hero™, Barry Spilchuk and Penny Tremblay

Resources

Barbara De Angelis, **www.barbaradeangelis.com**

BioPed, Crystal Kauffman, **www.bioped.ca**

BizLaunch, Andrew Patricio, **www.bizlaunch.ca**

Cal's Club,
   www.youthconnect.ca/htdocs/english/getinvolved/stories/calvin.asp

Callander Bay Dental Centre, **www.callanderbaydental.com**

Carte Blanche, David Lamothe, **www.carteblancheproducts.com**

Central Florida Urban League, **www.cful.org**

Cox Roofing, **www.CoxRoofing.com**

Dentistry Plus, Dr. Dennis Marangos, **www.altimadental.com**

For Better or For Worse, Lynn Johnston, **www.fborfw.com**

FreshBooks, Saul Colt, **www.freshbooks.com**

Harvey Mackay, **www.harveymackay.com**

Internal Rhythms Massage and Hydrotherapy Clinic, Vanessa Brown,
   www.internalrhythms.com
Jack Canfield, **www.jackcanfield.com**
Jordan Adler, **www.thecoolbuzz.com**
Kulik Dental, Dr. Darren Kulik, **www.kulikdental.com**
La Tienda, Raquel Sticklee, **www.latienda.ca**
Manifesting for Non-Gurus, Robert MacPhee,
   www.manifestingfornongurus.com
More Than Coffee, Nick Lamatrice, **www.morethancoffee.org**,
   www.morethancoffee.ca
Northern Computer Services, Graham Robinson, **www.northerncs.com**
Planned Television Arts, Rick Frishman, **www.rickfrishman.com**
Sellebration Productions, Kyle Selle, **www.yourspecialevent.ca**
SendOutCards, Kody Bateman, **www.sendoutcards.com**
Smiles For Life, **www.smilesforlife.org**
Stephen R. Covey, **www.stephencovey.com**
Strategy for Good, Susan Hyatt, **www.businessgivingstrategies.com**
THE cANCER DANCE, Barry Spilchuk, **www.THEcancerDANCE.com**
TOMS Shoes, Blake Mycoskie, **www.toms.com**,
Tremblay Leadership Center, Penny Tremblay, **www.pennytremblay.com**
Tri Thermal Roofing System™, Stan Cox, **www.ttrsystems.com**
Union of Ontario Indians, Maurice Switzer, **www.anishinabek.ca**
Zero Aids and ParticiPatrick, Christine Fortin, **www.Patrick4Life.org**

Journal of Thoughts to Give and Be Rich

_____

_____

_____

_____

_____

_____

_____

_____

_____

_____

_____

_____

_____

_____

_____

_____

_____

_____

_____

Journal of Thoughts to Give and Be Rich

_____
_____
_____
_____
_____
_____
_____
_____
_____
_____
_____
_____
_____
_____
_____
_____
_____
_____
_____
_____
_____
_____

Journal of Thoughts to Give and Be Rich

Journal of Thoughts to Give and Be Rich

Journal of Thoughts to Give and Be Rich

Journal of Thoughts to Give and Be Rich

_____

_____

_____

_____

_____

_____

_____

_____

_____

_____

_____

_____

_____

_____

_____

_____

_____

_____

_____

_____

_____

_____

Journal of Thoughts to Give and Be Rich

Journal of Thoughts to Give and Be Rich

9 781614 489467